God's Footprint on My Floor

God's Footprint on My Floor

By
Leo R. Van Dolson

1951

Southern Publishing Association
Nashville, Tennessee

Copyright © 1977 by
Southern Publishing Association
Library of Congress Catalog Card No. 76-56996
SBN 8127-0132-1

This book was
Edited by Richard Coffen
Designed by Dean Tucker
Photography by Dave Damer

Type set 11/13 Melior

Printed in U.S.A.

Dedication

To Bobbie Jane,
whose kindness and love to all
have helped me better
understand the love portrayed
in this volume

Contents

Chapter 1

What Everybody Ought to "No"

Pity the poor Pharisee. Pity him, of course, for his proverbial inability to see beyond his own nose. And pity him for his paradoxical capability of perceiving the fleck of dust in his brother's eye through the beam in his own. Pity him, too, for the pride and passion which he took in his own piety. But most of all, pity him for the little-recognized fact that he was a very good man, compared to the rogues and scoundrels that abounded in his day; yet he was not quite good enough.

Then imagine, if you can, the Pharisee's exquisite discomfiture on that catastrophic day which forever turned his well-ordered world upside down. It happened in an unlikely place too —a hillside above the little fishing village of Capernaum. And the words themselves came from the lips of an unlikely person—a Galilean peasant garbed in the simplest of robes. Yet His words brought the monumental building blocks of the pharisaic philosophical castle tumbling about the ears of those pridefully pious men.

They were such simple words: "I say unto you, That except your righteousness shall exceed the righteousness of the scribes and Pharisees, ye shall in no case enter into the kingdom of heaven" (Matthew 5:20). Absurd words. Unbelievable words. Who could possibly take them seriously?

Yet from the time those words were spoken, no one has ever quite taken the Pharisees as seriously as before. There they stood, exposed clearly in all their pretensions and self-proclaimed piety —exposed by the finger of God as not being good enough.

How cruel and unjust the charge must have seemed to the Pharisees that day! Hadn't they added innumerable statutes of their own to the Ten Commandments in order to preserve them and shore them up? They went to great lengths to determine every possible variation from the letter of the law and to fill in the breaches. They would argue endlessly over minor questions of interpretation and application. And now in the court of public opinion, Jesus made it obvious that all their thought and effort and human attempts to live according to the law were absurdly in vain.

Clearly and convincingly Jesus illustrated the Pharisees' vain strivings for man-made righteousness. Incisively His loving rebuke spotlighted the shallowness of their false assumptions. Six times Jesus of Nazareth drove the point home. *You say,* "Do not kill." But God's law goes much farther. It really tells you not to get angry, not to call people names, but to live in peace with all men. *You say,* "Don't commit adultery." But the law really instructs you not to lust or sin even by a thought. *You say,* "When a man puts away his wife, he must give her a written notice of divorce." That's not good enough! I say, "You are not to divorce at all except on grounds of marital infidelity." You say, "Don't break an oath sworn in the sight of God." But God doesn't want you to take an oath at all. You live by the principle "an eye for an eye and a tooth for a tooth." But God's standard of righteousness goes far beyond that. He says, "Don't resist if someone wants to harm you. If someone wants to sue you for the shirt off your back, don't go to court; give him your overcoat too. If an authority forces you to carry his burden one mile, gladly carry it two miles. Don't refuse anything to anyone who wants to beg or borrow from you." You say, "Love your friends and hate your enemies." My code of life is, "Love your enemies. Bless those who curse you. Pray for those who persecute you. You see, only when you can live this way are you really sons and daughters of your heavenly Father" (Matthew 5:21-48, paraphrased).

Imagine, if you can, the impact of Jesus' incisive interpretation of the Ten Commandments on those Pharisees who prided themselves in knowing and keeping God's laws. They felt shattered. Their whole complicated framework of life, the learned hagglings of their great rabbis, were forever exposed as not good enough.

All they could do was mumble, "That's ridiculous. Who does He think He is, trying to set us straight? That which He's asking is absolutely impossible. No one can be expected to live that way."

Yet they dimly realized that standing before

What Everybody Ought to "No"

them was One who did live that way. For months their spies had trailed Him, reporting His every word and action. They knew how Jesus lived, and they didn't dare accuse Him of hypocrisy.

They were right in a sense, however. None of us can live that way—unless he is born again, unless he is transformed by a miracle of grace, unless he learns to draw on the same Omnipotent Source that Jesus relied on. Yet the whole thrust of Christ's teaching that day on the mountain was not to show up the absurdity of the Pharisees' kind of religion or to discourage us from trying. He intended merely to challenge us with the possibility and to show us how we can be "perfect, even as . . . [our] Father which is in heaven is perfect" (verse 48).

It's not a magical kind of perfection, however. Jesus made it very plain that day. In the Beatitudes He taught us how to grow up after the new birth and how to submit ourselves fully to God's will. Then He went on to show us what we might become. He pointed to the Pharisees only to illustrate that what even the best of men can do is not good enough. God makes possible to His children something far better.

Therefore, Jesus explained, we must *know* the rules. Perfection is measured by God-given standards and fully understood only as God explains them to us. God's laws are not the requirements for getting into heaven but are, instead, the yardstick of our growing experience with Him.

We live today in an era sometimes called the Permissive Age. Even Dr. Spock has recently indicated that he's sorry for the results of the permissiveness he encouraged. Today the only no-no seems to be that which forbids no-nos. People have become so concerned about not damaging children's egos or inhibiting their creativity that they have seemingly forgotten all about developing children's characters.

At such a time as this, when Puritans are regarded as the bad guys, whereas the fiend who murders for fun is an overnight sensation, it's time to take a new look at the value of the old prohibitions. In our time of energy crisis it's obvious that laws which limit speed, regulate the flow of traffic and business transactions, dictate building codes, tax excessive profits, prescribe legal procedures, and legislate civil concerns are essential to the preservation of society and of our individual lives. Why not, then, admit that we need guidelines and regulations also in the moral and social relationships of man to man and man to God?

So at the top of the list of what everybody ought to "no" must of necessity be those rules which tear us down rather than enable us to know best how to live healthy, happy, and holy lives. Rules, for instance, that tell us not to eat too much, not to "burn the candle at both ends," are not restrictive no-nos; they are actually designed to provide the know-how essential to our experiencing something better than we might choose for ourselves without their help.

Of course, some of the bad press that the Ten Commandments have received in the years which have intervened since the Sermon on the Mount is due to the fact that many who have interpreted them have stressed the no-no aspect so much that they seem to have forgotten that God would rather say "yes-yes" to us.

In fact, when we carefully look at the Ten Commandments as God intended us to view them, we see that they are not really restrictions but word pictures of the kind of character His children will reflect when they choose to live as He would have them live. God never intended for the Ten Commandments to become a kind of football field where Pharisees can knock each other down into the mud. When we use the Ten Commandments correctly, they become a description of the converted person's character and a means of checking our progress in Christian growth. Let's take a new look, then, at these old laws, as we have outlined them in the diagram on page 15.

Thus we see from carefully studying this diagram that the laws the Creator has given us are made not to destroy us or to harm us but to help us achieve His kind of character. It's only natural, when we break these laws of life and health and begin to suffer the consequences of such violation, to blame someone or something else for our problems. Often we turn against the laws and try to make them the culprit rather than to take responsibility ourselves for the problems which result from our blatant violations of them.

At times we even turn against the Lawgiver and blame God, who desires only that we trust and obey in order that we may have the very best out of life. Anyone who keeps God's laws merely because he's *afraid not to,* serves God from wrong motives and

WORD PICTURE OF THE CONVERTED PERSON'S CHARACTER

1. LOYALTY—God must be first. If we are Christ's, our thoughts are of Him. We will seek the spiritual, not the material. We long to bear His image, breathe His Spirit, do His will, and please Him in all things.

2. WORSHIP—We worship the unseen, not the seen. The things we once hated we now love, and the things once loved we now hate. The soul is cleansed from vanity and pride and we have regular seasons of deep and earnest devotions.

3. REVERENCE—This forbids not only swearing and the secularization of the sacred, but also a false profession. The vain customs and fashions of the world are laid aside. Our conversation, affections, and sympathies are in heaven. The heart is kept tender and subdued by the Spirit of Christ.

4. SANCTIFICATION—Christ is recognized as Creator and Re-Creator, not only in the keeping of the seventh part of time, but in our full acceptance of the rest of redemption. His holiness is evidenced in our lives, and the works of holiness, which previously seemed dull, uninteresting, and wearisome, are now our delight.

5. RESPECT FOR AUTHORITY—This begins in the home between parents and children, but extends to all relationships with both God and man. Disobedience and rebellion are replaced by obedience and cooperation.

6. LOVE—Even hate and anger violate this commandment, but in the truly converted, love, humility, and peace take the place of anger, envy, and strife. The soul is imbued with divine love and captivated with the heavenly mysteries. The fruit of the Spirit—love—is evidenced in the life.

7. PURITY—There is a complete transformation—passion, appetites, and will are brought into perfect subjection. The former life appears disgusting and sinful. Sinful thoughts are put away and evil deeds renounced. Piety is evidenced at home and abroad.

8. HONESTY—This involves our relationship not only with our fellow-man, but with God. Instead of robbing God of such things as our health, time, tithe, and offerings, we gladly dedicate all we have to Him. Duty becomes a delight and sacrifice a pleasure.

9. TRUTHFULNESS—By our words we shall be justified or condemned. When the heart is right, words and deeds will be right and we shall become men and women of strict integrity. Self is subdued, and evil speaking is overcome.

10. CONTENTMENT—No longer shall we be jealous or discontented, because our lives are not centered on the material. The practice of holiness will be pleasant when there is perfect surrender to God. Joy takes the place of sadness, and the countenance reflects the peace and happiness of heaven.

cheats himself out of gaining all that God really wants him to have. This is made plain in the Old Testament gospel story portrayed in the moving experiences of the prophet Hosea.

Hosea learned through his tragic marriage to a woman who became undeserving and immoral how far-reaching and all-encompassing God's love and compassion are. "When Israel was a child, I loved him, and out of Egypt I called my son. The more I called them, the more they went from me; they kept sacrificing to the Baals, and burning incense to idols. Yet it was I who taught Ephraim to walk, I took them up in my arms; but they did not know that I healed them. I led them with cords of compassion, with the bands of love, and I became to them as one who eases the yoke on their jaws, and I bent down to them and fed them" (Hosea 11:1-4, RSV).

Despite our handicaps, despite the deformities of sin, God *wants* us. That's what Hosea 11 is talking about! "When Israel was a child, I loved him, and out of Egypt I called my son."

But notice the strange reaction of Israel, and then ask yourself, "Is this *my attitude*? Is this the way I, too, react to Christ's compassionate love?" "The more I called them, the more they went from me; they kept sacrificing to the Baals, and burning incense to idols. Yet it was I who taught Ephraim to walk, I took them up in my arms; but they did not know that I healed them."

The fourth verse brings God's answer to human carelessness and backslidings: "I led them with cords of compassion, with the bands of love, and

I became to them as one who eases the yoke on their jaws, and I bent down to them and fed them."

God bends down in compassion and interest, but His people are bent in another direction. "My people are bent on turning away from me; so they are appointed to the yoke, and none shall remove it" (verse 7, RSV).

In spite of it all, God longingly pleads: "How can I give you up, O Ephraim! How can I hand you over, O Israel! How can I make you like Admah! How can I treat you like Zeboiim! My heart recoils within me, my compassion grows warm and tender" (verse 8, RSV).

Admah and Zeboiim were cities God destroyed along with Sodom and Gomorrah. God doesn't want to visit His fierce judgments on His people. He cries, "How can I give you up? . . . My heart recoils within me, my compassion grows warm and tender." The all-embracing compassion, forgiveness, and love of Christ reach out to us, no matter how we reject and neglect Him.

Here is love that truly will not let us go. Yet God cannot force us to receive His love!

Why does God love us? Why does He agonize over us? I don't know! There certainly is no advantage to Him in loving us, but on the cross, Jesus clearly demonstrated that God's love is not selfish like man's. Often men love only when it is to their advantage to do so. But even before the cross was fully placed, while rough soldiers were still driving the nails through His wrists, Jesus prayed, "Father, forgive them; for they know not what they do" (Luke 23:34).

What Everybody Ought to "No"

That's God's kind of love—not man's! That's what He tells us in Hosea 11:9, RSV: "I will not execute my fierce anger, I will not again destroy Ephraim; for I am God and not man, the Holy One in your midst, and I will not come to destroy."

"I am God and not man." In no way is the superiority of God's character better seen than in His willingness to forgive even the most grievous sins. Christ's warm, tender, all-embracing compassion, when truly understood and received, becomes a *compelling force* in our lives. It is our love in response to His love which alone can *truly* motivate Christian obedience.

"I led them with cords of compassion, with the bands of love, and I became to them as one who eases the yoke on their jaws, and I bent down to them and fed them" (verse 4, RSV). He binds us with the bands of love, with cords of compassion, and *He will never let us go!* As long as we *choose* to abide in His forgiveness, as long as our hearts fully respond to His love with loving Christian service, nothing—*nothing at all*—can break the cords of love that bind us to Him!

After all, we don't really sin against *law,* do we? We sin against a relationship. We break the cords of love God has woven about us. Sin is not just breaking a written code that God originally inscribed a long time ago on tables of stone. If it were, it would be rather adventuresome to try to get away with something once in a while without getting caught. But sin is the breaking of God's loving heart, and it isn't fun to break someone's heart. When we sin, we are turning our backs on

God's Footprint on My Floor

God, and He suffers anew the agony of rejection which Christ felt when those He had come to save spit on Him and when His dearest friends ran away. *But more*—when we sin, God suffers the indescribable agony of the parent who sees his child ruining his life and refusing the loving guidance of one who desires only his best good.

It was this concept of the compelling power of love that Christ attempted to clarify in the Sermon on the Mount when He blessed those who reflect God's tender love and compassion but refused to bless the Pharisees, who had just about taken all the happiness and understanding out of service to God. There is not a word in the Beatitudes about being blessed or happy by strict pharisaical obedience to the commandments. This was so obvious to the Pharisees—who were listening critically to everything Jesus said—that they were about to accuse Him of doing away with God's law. But Jesus read their hearts, and before they had a chance to attack Him publicly on the issue, He said, " 'Think not that I have come to abolish the law and the prophets; I have come not to abolish them but to fulfil them' " (Matthew 5:17, RSV).

Fulfill means to live them and put them in their proper perspective, as we see in the verses which follow: "For truly, I say to you, till heaven and earth pass away, not an iota, not a dot, will pass from the law until all is accomplished. Whoever then relaxes one of the least of these commandments and teaches men so, shall be called least in the kingdom of heaven; but he who does them and teaches them shall be called great in the kingdom

What Everybody Ought to "No"

of heaven" (Matthew 5:18, 19, RSV).

What *is* Christ doing in these verses? He is contrasting true righteousness with false righteousness. Then He goes on in His sermon to illustrate His point with the six selections from the Books of the Law to which we referred earlier.

Let's look at them again, this time in chart form to help us get the full impact of Christ's purpose.

Matt 5 verses	What Pharisees Taught	What Christ Taught
verses 21-26	"Thou shalt not kill."	Don't even get angry.
verses 27-30	"Thou shalt not commit adultery."	Don't even lust.
verses 31, 32	Give wife a certificate of divorce.	No divorce, except for unfaithfulness.
verses 33-37	Do not swear falsely.	Don't swear at all.
verses 38-42	"An eye for an eye, and a tooth for a tooth."	Don't resist anyone who is evil. Turn the other cheek.
verses 43-47	Love your neighbor and hate your enemy.	"Love your enemies, bless them that curse you, do good to them that hate you, and pray for them which despitefully use you."

As you look at these comparisons again, ask yourself who was really stricter—Christ or the Pharisees? Which way is the most difficult to follow? Obviously, Christ's way—the way of love —is. That is, it's difficult when we try to do it on our own. That's what was the matter with the Pharisees. They were trying too hard. In fact, they tried so hard that, by their own admission, they added 1,521 laws to only one of the ten which God gave. They spent their lives trying to remember all the minutia so they would know what to do in each life situation. But it was impossible. God doesn't work that way, nor does He expect man to!

Jesus climaxed His explanation that the righteousness of the Pharisees was not good enough by challenging: "Be ye therefore perfect, even as your Father which is in heaven is perfect" (Matthew 5:48).

We too are prone to do just what we pictured the Pharisees doing—that is, throwing their hands up in the air and shaking their heads as they muttered, "It's impossible!" That's exactly what Jesus wants to impress upon us. It's absolutely impossible for man, no matter how hard he tries, to live in full accord with God's laws. Only as we take the steps Christ outlines in the Beatitudes, only as we become sons and daughters of the Heavenly King, only as we submit ourselves in full surrender to His will and allow His life, compassion, and beauty of character to be seen in us can we become as perfect in our sphere as God is in His (see *Testimonies for the Church*, Vol. 8, p. 64). It's not anything *we* do, but what *God* does in us.

It may seem amusing to play with sin, but after a while we wake up to the fact that sin is a loathsome cancer that permeates the whole system, disgracing and disfiguring its victim. Sin robs life of everything God intended it to be.

Surgery is the only way to get rid of the cancer

of sin, and fortunately we have a Great Physician who has never lost a patient who fully entrusted himself to His care. Some have *preferred to die* from cancer rather than to risk surgery, and strangely a large number are afraid to come to Christ for healing from the cancer of sin because such healing demands surgery of the soul. However, there is no other way. No do-it-yourself home remedy can remove the cancerous growth of evil that threatens to destroy the soul.

Jeremiah illustrates man's inability to remove his own sin: " 'Though you wash yourself with lye and use much soap, the stain of your guilt is still before me, says the Lord God' " (Jeremiah 2:22, RSV). Why can't we remove the stains of sin ourselves? They go too deep. They permeate our whole being. The situation is grave. The remedy must be drastic. It demands a new life, and this *we cannot obtain by ourselves*. Only the God who created life in the first place has power to re-create us in His image and to remove sin and wrong from our lives.

First, as the Beatitudes point out, we must realize our need. But how can we sense our sinfulness? Paul answers, "I had not known sin, but by the law" (Romans 7:7). God's law is not our savior. Instead it is the mirror (see James 1:23-25) which reveals our hopelessness and our need. It won't do any good to break the mirror or throw it aside. Our sin would still remain. God's law points out our need and thus leads us to the One who can supply that need. The law reveals God's standard of perfection and righteousness. It sets forth the

God's Footprint on My Floor

eternal principles of love (Matthew 22:37-40). Yet we fall short of such perfection. We cannot meet the claims of God's holy law. But Christ can. That's why He came and lived among men. He didn't come just to die for our sins. He lived a holy life and developed a perfect character, which He offers us in exchange for our lives of sin.

Christ never forces us to accept the imprint of His character. Instead He leads us with the cords of compassion and binds us with the bonds of love. Through these ties He helps us *want* to do that which sheer determination is powerless to accomplish.

Now what about you and me? Are our affections centered on Jesus Christ? Have we found the happiness of those who are truly blessed? Do we love our Lord so much that we are bound to Him by cords of love that will not let us go? Are our lives testimonies to the happiness, peace, and victory of the Christian way? Are we reflecting as fully as we should the beauty of Christ's character and the fullness of His love? That is our privilege. That is what Matthew 5 tells us Jesus makes possible, and what this book is all about.

Fred Fisher, who had served as bishop of India for ten years, and who was a good friend of Ghandi, loved all men for what they were. His life fully demonstrated Christ's love and compassion. His last pastorate was the Methodist Central Church in Detroit, Michigan; on a bronze plaque in the sanctuary of that church is inscribed a portion of a poem written about him by a friend, Sir Rabindranath Tagore, an Indian poet-philosopher.

What Everybody Ought to "No"

Frederick Bohn Fisher

Bishop   Missionary   Preacher

*"And when you had taken your leave,
I found God's footprint on my floor."*

How can we have this kind of experience? How can we actually live so close to Christ and so fully reflect His character that we leave His footprint on the floor of those places we visit? The chapters which follow attempt to focus clearly on Christ's own answer to this all-important question.

God's Footprint on My Floor

A Voice With a Difference

Many voices beckon to us with the siren song "Come here and see what we have to offer." Everything from soap ads to blurbs for pleasure cruises promise us much but deliver precious little. We take medicine to get over the results of something we'd taken for what ailed us in the first place. Antibiotics sometimes kill weak bacteria, leaving the strong ones to get us down. Automobiles create bumper-to-bumper traffic jams, which make it impossible to go places. Automatic dishwashers leave the glasses and silver spotted. Even our vacations to exotic spots around the globe leave us so fatigued we can hardly drag ourselves back to work. Consequently, we've become skeptical.

Similarly, when Jesus delivered the Sermon on the Mount, there were many teachers, even as there are now, who stated, "Many paths lead to the reality of life and truth." Even then Rabbi Wise and Doctor Philosophy and Guru Mystic all hypothesized that there is truth in each approach to life. "Take your choice," they suggested. "There's more than one way to look at things. Truth has many facets." And the more the people listened, the more difficult it was to know what to believe.

However, the voice from the Mount of Beatitudes was a voice with a difference. It phrased ideas in simple language that everyone could understand. Jesus spoke with conviction and with the authority of Heaven. Because truth carries its own verification, the people who listened to that voice recognized the simplicity and beauty of eternal truth. "Never man spake like this man," they exclaimed.

Today that voice from the Galilean hillside echoes across a span of nearly two thousand years, but it carries the same conviction and clarity. We, too, as we listen are moved with awe and admiration. There is no pussyfooting here, no equivocating. With the assurance that He is God's own Son sent to lead mankind out of darkness into the light of truth, Christ challenges our thoughtful attention with the most earthshaking claims of all—"I *am* the way. I *am* the truth. I *am* the life. No one can come to God in any other way except by *Me*" (see John 14:6).

In words all could understand and treasure, Christ on the Mount of Blessing outlined seven simple steps for those who want to become God's sons and daughters—the way we can ever fulfill the challenge of becoming so like Him that everywhere we go we shall leave not our footprints but His on the floor.

The first several verses of Matthew 5 contain Christ's answer to such pressing problems of life as pride and insecurity, sin and guilt, despair and disillusionment. The Beatitudes offer a line of

God's Footprint on My Floor

progression that leads us step by step to the kind of happiness and peace which come from the realization that we are truly God's sons and daughters.

In the chapters which follow we shall study God's answers to life's problems as we delineate the simple program Christ Himself outlined for us. Here I must say with all the forcefulness and clarity at my disposal that this is God's program and not mine—and it works. I've seen His power at work, and I know what He has done, is doing, and will continue to do for people just like you and me. We need not be chips tossed around in the sea of fate. Even in this age of novelty, change, and future shock God guides our lives and will gladly teach us His way to peace, happiness, and the more abundant life.

The Bible tells us that in the beginning God made mankind and the earth just as perfect as a loving, all-powerful Creator could. But when Adam and Eve transgressed the laws God had made for their benefit and happiness, the sin that resulted was an all-pervasive, full-blown, 4-D evil —disease, despair, death, and decay. However, even in a world which shows the degenerating effects of sin, we can still find evidences of God's love which cause us to pause and wonder at our Creator's thoughtfulness and imagination. In addition, the deepest and tenderest ties of earthly love, although imperfect representations, also help us appreciate God's love for us.

The greatest revelation of God's love, however, is seen in the price He willingly paid to redeem us after we had fallen in sin. "For God so loved the world, that he gave his only begotten Son, that whosoever believeth in him should not perish, but have everlasting life" (John 3:16). Jesus lived and suffered and died to redeem us. John, who wrote this favorite text, also summarizes the message of the Bible in just three words: "God is love" (1 John 4:8). If we really appreciate that text, it will make all the difference in the way we live and relate to the happenings in our world. Jesus became "a man of sorrows" so that we might partake of His everlasting joy.

Dwight L. Moody tells of the time that he was building a house in Chicago for workingmen. A businessman said, "I would like to put up a text on the wall that you are building." Moody agreed, thinking that he simply wanted to write out a motto. But one day he found a gasman working back of the pulpit. "What are you doing there?" Moody demanded. He found out that the text was being installed in gas jets. In those days gas illuminated the buildings, so they could not light that hall without lighting the text. For years Moody preached there with the text blazing behind him and burning into the hearts and minds of the people who came to that hall: "God is love."

A man shuffling by looked in through the door and saw that text, "God is love." "God is *not* love," he muttered. But by and by the man returned and looked at the gas-jet Bible verse again.

Moody recounts, "I saw the man go in and sit down by the door, and before I knew it, he had his hands up to his face. Once in a while I would see tears run down. I was interested, foolishly thinking

God's Footprint on My Floor

that it was due to my preaching. I got down by the door before he went out, and I said, 'What's the trouble?'

"He said confusedly, 'I don't know.' When God gets hold of a man, he can't always tell what it means. Some men are cross and ugly to their wives; others fight with men, fight the church members, fight with the ungodly.

"I got into the pew with this particular man and I said, 'What was in the sermon that made you cry?' but he said he didn't even know that I had been preaching, and didn't know anything about the sermon. I was floored. Well, was it something that had been read? Was it anything in the songs? He couldn't remember anything in the songs. 'What is the matter?' I urged insistently.

"He glanced upward and said, 'That text up there.'

"I said, 'Man, believe God loves you.'

"He said, 'I ain't worth loving.'

" 'That's true,' I said. 'But he loves you all the same.' And I sat there a half an hour, and we got it down into his soul and I had reason afterward to know that divine grace wrought its wondrous work in him, and he became a new man" (D. L. Moody, *God Is Love*, p. 32).

Oh, that we could only realize the meaning and reality of God's love for us! In all that He does, God has the well-being of His children in view. He has something far better in mind for you than you are seeking for yourself. He knows what is best for each of us and plans for the good of those whom He loves.

A Voice With a Difference

Many of us feel troubled, concerned, and anxious in this worrisome age of future shock. We worry about failure, worry about our children, and fret about what's going to happen next in our world. But we need not fear. God loves us and cares for us. He is planning a wonderful future for us and urges us to place all our worries, anxieties, and concerns in His all-powerful hands. He offers peace and happiness to those who will accept His love and yield their lives to Him.

And 1 Peter 5:7 should describe your appreciative response: "Casting all . . . [my] care upon him; for he careth for . . . [me]."

God's Footprint on My Floor

CHRIST'S ANSWER TO MAN'S NEED

(Based on the Beatitudes in Matthew 5)

OUR PROBLEM	CHRIST'S ANSWER	RESULTS
	(Blessed are . . .)	

1. PRIDE   INSECURITY
    POOR SELF-IMAGE
	*THE POOR IN SPIRIT
	   Those who recognize their need and
	   begin to do something about it
		*Acceptance of self
		*Conquest of false pride
		*Meaningful communion
		  with God and man

Chapter 3

Giants Aren't Sanforized

Sometimes giants see themselves as pygmies, and sometimes pygmies view themselves as giants. In both cases, the self-image is so twisted that the individual involved cannot face the realities of life. Obviously, in this sort of situation, one extreme is just as bad as the other.

A skillful brain surgeon tells how he was called in for consultation in the case of a child who needed surgery. Although he didn't perform the operation, he did stand by in case his expertise was needed. As a result of the operation the child lived. The day after surgery the mother came to the surgeon's office and insisted on seeing him. As she expressed her gratitude, she shyly held out to him a small cloth purse which undoubtedly she herself had made.

The surgeon, offended at what he thought was an attempt to pay for his services with a humble gift not worthy of his talents, mouthed, "I'm sorry, but my secretary will bill you for the amount of my fee. I really have no use for this purse, although I appreciate your making it for me."

The woman, without appearing offended, quietly asked him what his fee would be. "Oh, the least I could settle for would be two hundred dollars. After all, you see, I . . ." Quickly the woman reached into the homemade purse, peeled off two of the five one hundred dollar bills it contained, placed them on his desk, and walked out of the office.

On the other side of the coin the Bible relates a story that tells how a whole group of people under-rated their possibilities. After two years of preserv-ing the large army of Hebrew people who had come from Egypt through a remarkable series of provi-dences, God led them to the borders of the Promised Land. In preparation for the initial invasion, Moses sent twelve men to spy out the land of Canaan. After an itinerary of forty days, they returned, laden down with huge clusters of grapes, figs, and pomegranates. Just as the Israelites were about to express their enthusiasm for possessing the land, ten of the spies began to paint a very pessimistic picture: "The land, through which we have gone to search it, is a land that eateth up the inhabitants thereof; and all the people that we saw in it are men of a great stature. And there we saw the giants, . . . and we were in our own sight as grasshoppers, and so we were in their sight" (Numbers 13:32, 33).

The majority's report disheartened the people, and they promptly forgot how God had led and pre-served them. All they could think about were the giants and how they were "grasshoppers" in com-parison. Consequently the Israelites didn't go into Canaan. Instead they wandered in the wilderness another forty years. Their children, who saw things

Giants Aren't Sanforized

in the proper perspective, went in and possessed the land. The giants didn't seem so big to them; they found, as one of my favorite preachers likes to put it, that giants aren't Sanforized but can be shrunk down to size.

Most of our problems come from the fact that we, like the Israelites, have a hard time assessing ourselves accurately. Our problems often center around the distorted self-images we have built from our pride or insecurity. Such false self-images tend to defeat our attempts to get the most out of life and to relate properly to the real world.

But giants aren't Sanforized, so it's most important to discover for ourselves that whatever the giant is in the way of our living in God's Promised Land, it, too, can be shrunk down to size.

The first step in shrinking the giant of a distorted self-image down to size, whether we feel too egotistic or too inferior, is a willingness to face ourselves as we really are. It is, of course, traumatic for most of us to see ourselves as others see us. Robert Burns, while sitting in church, watched a louse crawling on a lady in the next pew and received the inspiration for his famous poem entitled "To a Louse." The most remembered line of that poem is, in modern English, "Oh, would some power this gift now give us, to see ourselves as others see us." But very few know Burns' next words: "It would from many a blunder free us, and foolish notion."

Most of us realize our need for improvement, but many of us actually undervalue ourselves because we lack a sanctified sense of self-respect.

God's Footprint on My Floor

Jesus challenged Christians to love their neighbors as they love themselves (Matthew 22:39). Christian psychiatrists tell us that if we don't have a proper sense of self-respect, we will be unable to really love God or our neighbor.

Yet many of us feel guilty about having any kind of self-respect. We see it as a form of selfishness, because we're used to singing such hymns as: "Alas! and did my Saviour bleed?/And did my Sovereign die?/Would He devote that sacred head/For such a worm as I?" That last line doesn't contribute much to our self-image, does it?

Or what about the second stanza of the old version of "Beneath the Cross of Jesus"? "And from my smitten heart with tears/Two wonders I confess:/The wonders of redeeming love/And my own worthlessness." The last word in most modern versions reads "unworthiness" instead of "worthlessness." That's a little better, for certainly we are "unworthy"; but how can we consider ourselves "worthless" when God gave all to redeem us?

The tendency among Christians to make a virtue out of excessive humility means that they are not able to honestly encounter God, other human beings, or even themselves. Robert Burton in his *Anatomy of Melancholy* wrote of those who "are proud in humility, proud in that they are not proud."

Often an attitude of superiority masks a lack of self-esteem. Psychologists tell us that there is no such thing as a superiority complex. What appears to be inordinate boasting is really a cover for inadequate feelings.

Giants Aren't Sanforized

Since we tend to see in others what we see in ourselves, we project the attitudes and actions we don't like in ourselves into what those about us are doing. Hence the more we condemn in ourselves, the more difficult it will be to get along with others.

An old Quaker used to sit by the public well in a village square to watch the settlers heading west. One day a stranger who had stopped to water his team spouted, "I'm looking for a new place to move my family. Where I used to live, people were cold, unneighborly, and hard to get along with. So I moved."

The old man replied, "Thou wilt find it about the same way here."

Later another stranger said, "I dreaded to move. Our neighbors were kind and friendly. To leave them was a grief of heart to me."

Whereupon the old man observed, "Thou wilt find it about the same way here."

A bystander who had overheard both conversations challenged the Quaker: "How is it you tell strangers that we are both unfriendly and friendly?"

"That I did not do," the old man responded. "I said: 'Thou wilt find it about the same way here.' And 'tis true. The first man always will have bad neighbors, and the second man always will have good neighbors. A man makes his own neighbors."

We have to be careful about what is being said here. It's easy to misunderstand. The Christian's acceptance of himself as God's son or daughter is in no way self-centered. We get mixed up between the concepts of status and self-respect. Status is concerned with how we stand in comparison with

God's Footprint on My Floor

others and should not concern a Christian.

Yet what do the Scriptures mean when they challenge the Christian to "deny himself, and take up his cross" (Matthew 16:24)? What does it mean to crucify self?

Psychologists tell us that the favorable attitudes and treatment by those who mean the most to us strongly influence our self-esteem. For this reason we ought to use our influence to enhance one another. But think for a moment of Christ. He was misunderstood, persecuted, and finally put to death as the most shameful of criminals. He was often falsely accused, and at the height of His popularity the crowds turned against Him because He would not cater to their whims. He had no home for security and hardly anything in the way of worldly belongings. The garments He wore testified to His humble origins in the Galilean mountain village of Nazareth.

Most people came to Him because they thought He might do something for them, not because His status or position in life attracted them. Finally His closest friends forsook Him, and His enemies beat Him and spat upon Him. Even when He was being nailed to the cross, He prayed for those who caused Him such pain. No one did much to enhance Christ's ego and status through favorable attitudes or awards, yet He did not permit their snubs and cruelty, flattery or cursing, to thwart His life purpose.

How could a human being, so indifferent to status and ego needs, still love and respect people and show them such compassion as He did? Christ recognized Himself as the Son of God. He did not live for self but for the glory of God. He didn't need to defend Himself from the attacks and criticism of His peers, for His life centered not in self but in His relationship with God. Our desperate search for self-esteem stems from our self-centeredness. But when God is the center of our lives, self finds a new reason for being that lifts us out of the narrow, selfish plane of sinful existence to that of being God's children.

It is true, however, that before we can place God at the center of our beings, we must take self off the throne. We must understand that God's way will bring us true happiness, true security, and a sense of self-worth and self-fulfillment far beyond anything we could have experienced through building a positive self-image on our own.

Notice in the accompanying illustration that when self is at the center and "I" is on the throne, we wear the armor of defensiveness. It doesn't take us very long before we start building defense barriers about us to keep from having our egos destroyed.

However, when Christ takes over in our lives, He becomes our defense and security. We recognize our true individual worth as God's sons and daughters, and nothing can ever destroy our peace as long as our lives center in Him. Thus we don't need the walls of defensiveness. We're no longer concerned about threats to our status or ego, but with self secure in Christ we can reach out to share with others the same security in Christ we've found for ourselves.

God's Footprint on My Floor

WITH CHRIST AT THE CENTER

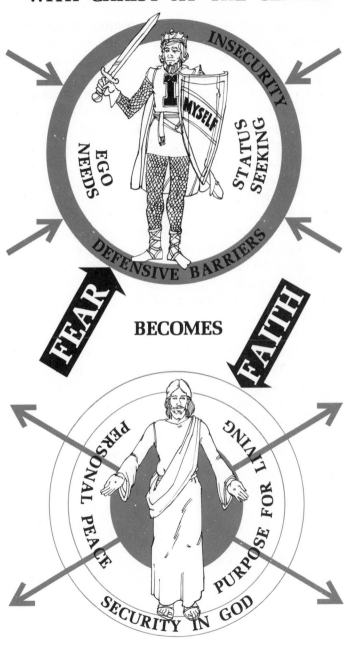

INSECURITY

EGO NEEDS

STATUS SEEKING

MYSELF

DEFENSIVE BARRIERS

FEAR   BECOMES   FAITH

PERSONAL PEACE

PURPOSE FOR LIVING

SECURITY IN GOD

God wants us to catch a glimpse of our need for Him and to experience the new life that will enable us to live as did Jesus. By His gracious provision we can live without the defense mechanisms that keep our egos from being destroyed.

This is why in the first Beatitude Jesus blessed those who are poor in spirit. "He opened his mouth, and taught them, saying, Blessed are the poor in spirit: for their's is the kingdom of heaven" (Matthew 5:2, 3).

Jesus was not talking about the person who has a poor self-image. Instead He was referring to those who recognize that Heaven sees nothing good in them. They know that all they have ever done has been mingled with selfishness and sin.

It's popular today to sneer at sin. Some even consider it an old-fashioned concept that doesn't belong in the space age. Yet everyone everywhere, whether he'll admit it or not, acknowledges its presence. Do you have a key in your pocket or purse? Why? Because of sin. If it weren't for sin, there wouldn't be any crime or any need of keys. Your banker may never have thought much about the theological implications of sin, but the moment you approach him for a loan, he's immediately aware of the practical consequences. Because it's a sinful world, he makes sure that he's protecting himself from being cheated.

Sin coils about all of us like a deadly viper, and it fastens its fangs in our souls and fills us with a poison that will destroy our hearts when we aren't even aware of it.

Because of sin our noble powers and well-

God's Footprint on My Floor

balanced minds have been perverted. Selfishness has taken the place of love. And now we find it difficult to respect or live with ourselves.

It is impossible for us, of ourselves, to escape. Jeremiah 2:22 plainly states, "Though thou wash thee with nitre, and take thee much soap, yet thine iniquity is marked before me, saith the Lord God." Paul adds, "The carnal mind is enmity against God: for it is not subject to the law of God, neither indeed can be" (Romans 8:7).

Ellen G. White's book *Steps to Christ* tells us, "Education, culture, the exercise of the will, human effort, all have their proper sphere, but here they are powerless. They may produce an outward correctness of behavior, but they cannot change the heart; they cannot purify the springs of life. There must be a power working from within, a new life from above, before men can be changed from sin to holiness. That power is Christ. His grace alone can quicken the lifeless faculties of the soul, and attract it to God, to holiness.

"The Saviour said, 'Except a man be born from above,' unless he shall receive a new heart, new desires, purposes, and motives, leading to a new life, 'he cannot see the kingdom of God.' John 3:3, margin. The idea that it is necessary only to develop the good that exists in man by nature, is a fatal deception. 'The natural man receiveth not the things of the Spirit of God: for they are foolishness unto him: neither can he know them, because they are spiritually discerned.' 'Marvel not that I said unto thee, Ye must be born again.' 1 Corinthians 2:14; John 3:7. Of Christ it is written, 'In Him was life;

Giants Aren't Sanforized

and the life was the light of men'—the only 'name under heaven given among men, whereby we must be saved.' John 1:4; Acts 4:12" (pages 18, 19).

When we are truly poor in spirit, we shall admit that we can't do anything to save ourselves, and thus we shall value the help that only Christ can bring. Once we realize the terrible nature of sin —how it is hurting and destroying us—then we will turn to Jesus for salvation.

The great giants of sin are attempting to keep us from the Promised Land—from our glorious birthright as God's sons and daughters. But these giants aren't Sanforized!

The young man David descended the slopes of the valley of Elah, defeated the giant Goliath, and brought back Goliath's head as a trophy of victory. The story has always thrilled young and old alike, but it appears that David was a prophetic type of Jesus, who later descended the slopes of death to grapple with the prince of evil. Having gained the victory for us, Jesus rose again, and in the power of His endless life He lives to represent us before His Father's throne.

Despite our sin, God has made it possible for us not only to be born again but also to grow up as children of the King. His power enabling us daily to become more like Him is attested in 2 Corinthians 3:18: "But all of us who are Christians have no veils on our faces, but reflect like mirrors the glory of the Lord. We are transfigured in ever-increasing splendor into his own image" (Phillips). It *is* possible for us to live so that wherever we step we leave Christ's footprint on the floor.

God's Footprint on My Floor

Therefore, we need not consider ourselves as "worms." Christians are new creatures being transformed by God's grace into His image, and someday our newness will be complete in Him. "Beloved, we are God's children now; it does not yet appear what we shall be, but we know that when he appears we shall be like him, for we shall see him as he is" (1 John 3:2, RSV).

Giants Aren't Sanforized

CHRIST'S ANSWER TO MAN'S NEED

(Based on the Beatitudes in Matthew 5)

OUR PROBLEM	CHRIST'S ANSWER	RESULTS
1. PRIDE INSECURITY POOR SELF-IMAGE	(Blessed are . . .) * THE POOR IN SPIRIT Those who recognize their need and begin to do something about it	* Acceptance of self * Conquest of false pride * Meaningful communion with God and man
2. SIN AND GUILT	* THEY THAT MOURN Repentance for and turning from sin	* Clear conscience * Evidence of acceptance by God and man

Give Your Guilt Away

You and I have a problem that is universal. It makes people miserable in Toronto as well as in Tokyo. It eats away at the heart of men and women in the Swiss Alps as well as on the edge of the Sahara. An *epidemic of guilt envelops our world.*

We are constantly caught between groups which hold standards or ideals that differ from ours. Our own conscience constantly clashes with the desires of the carnal nature, thus bringing about mountains of guilt. An infinite list of tiny guilts, such as not turning the lights off in the house or not stopping to pick up a tin can along the street, pesters us no end. In fact, some people feel miserable because they can't think of anything specific to feel guilty about. All this leaves us feeling as lost and confused and hopeless as an old plastic bottle bobbing in the middle of the ocean.

Although each of us possesses some guilt feelings, we should recognize that there are two kinds of guilt—abnormal guilt and normal guilt. On the one hand, abnormal guilt is destructive rather than constructive, for its poison can drive people to mental derangement and even suicide. On the other hand, normal guilt is helpful and healthy if we relate to it properly, for it can spur us to better habits and attitudes.

Abnormal guilt can sometimes cause physical disorders. A twenty-four-year-old pilot's arm became paralyzed the day after he flew on a bombing mission. The physicians could actually stick pins in it without his feeling them. During his childhood he had hit his sister in a fit of anger and had caused an impairment in her hearing. Somehow the bombing attack reactivated his buried sense of guilt, which manifested itself in the paralysis of the arm he had used to strike his sister.

Abnormal guilt is exaggerated clear out of proportion and often results from our inability to forgive ourselves or to believe in or accept the forgiveness of others. Once we recognize abnormal guilt for what it is, however, we can put it into its proper perspective and begin to deal with it as we would with normal guilt.

Nearly all thinking people, whether they accept God or not, agree that the universe operates under dependable natural laws. We as human beings function under these laws, which God—who knows what is best for us to do and not to do—made for us. These laws reach into every phase of our being —physical, mental, social, and spiritual—and the way we relate to them determines whether or not we are healthy and whole.

As pointed out previously, if these laws were arbitrary rules which we could harmlessly break, it would be rather exciting to try to get away with something. But instead, they help us know how to

Give Your Guilt Away

get the most out of life, and when we break them, we injure ourselves and usually others as well. Actually we don't *break* divine laws, but we break ourselves *on* them.

Therefore it's good for us to feel guilty if we lie, cheat, steal, slander others, or do those things which are contrary to the laws of life and health. Guilt is a mental pain which, like physical pain, warns us that something is wrong and that if we keep on doing the "something," we'll hurt ourselves badly.

That's why, in the Beatitude we're studying in this chapter, Jesus says, "Blessed are they that mourn: for they shall be comforted." He's not saying "Happy are those who are sad." That would be a contradiction. All the Beatitudes in Matthew 5 deal with spiritual needs, and Jesus refers here to sorrow for sin. When we feel guilty about wrongdoing, some well-meaning person might counsel us to forget it because we really haven't done anything wrong after all. Such advice might be helpful in the case of some abnormal guilt feeling, but trying to suppress guilt just doesn't work when we have violated the divinely established laws that govern our life and health. To pay no attention to these would be like driving right through barriers, warning signs, and flashing yellow lights erected on a freeway because the overpass just ahead has collapsed. For me to ignore normal guilt feelings is to admit deep down inside that I'm the kind of person who can lie or cheat or steal. This doesn't help me; it just leads to deterioration of character.

So we need to do something about guilt. But

God's Footprint on My Floor

what? A lot of people don't follow Christ's suggestion in the Beatitude we're studying, but try to establish mechanisms of their own for ridding themselves of guilt. Usually these methods involve some kind of physical torture that makes them feel they've paid penance for their sins—a far harsher way than God's plan for giving away our guilt.

In Singapore individuals will walk barefoot through red-hot coals to pay penance for things they consider to be wrong. Some beat themselves, as Martin Luther is said to have done, in order to get rid of guilt feelings. Others wash in rivers or make long pilgrimages to holy places to rid themselves of the taint of sin. All these are substitutes for God's plan of forgiveness.

When Jesus said, "Blessed are they that mourn," He meant that those who repent of sin are happy because they will find His comfort, His forgiveness, His method of removing guilt. Repentance includes not only sorrow for sin but a willingness to turn from it. In order to do this we must see sin for what it really is—that which robs life of all that God intended it to be. Until we really sorrow for sin, until we actually turn away from it in our hearts, there will be no real change in the life, no matter what we do outwardly to show penance.

The Bible tells the story of a wealthy ruler by the name of Nicodemus who came to Jesus at night to talk with the popular young teacher because he sensed his need of having the same freedom from guilt that Jesus had. He needed the freshness of the Holy Spirit in His life to blow out the cobwebs of sin.

Give Your Guilt Away

As the flutter of leaves in the moonlight accentuated the soft breeze, Jesus saw Nicodemus coming and greeted him pleasantly. Soon the conversation got around to the real reason Nicodemus had searched out Jesus, and the earnest voice of the Galilean Teacher penetrated to the very depths of Nicodemus' heart, telling him, "Unless you are born again, you can't see heaven."

"But, Lord, how can that be? Born again at my age? Can a person be born again after he has grown up? Surely you don't mean I can return to my mother and be born a second time."

Jesus quietly spoke again, "The truth is, only those born with water and the Spirit ever enter the kingdom of God. Being born of the flesh and being born of the Spirit are simply not the same! Don't look so surprised because I'm telling you that you need to be born again. Feel the wind quietly blowing. Listen to the sound of it in the branches of the trees. You can hear the wind. But tell Me, where did it come from? Where is it going? You don't know? Yet the Spirit brings the new birth in this same way!"

Jesus' words shocked the Pharisee to the depths of his soul. "You mean that in spite of all I've done I'm not good enough for heaven?"

Jesus explained clearly what it means to find freedom from sin and to be truly born again.

"In the interview with Nicodemus, Jesus unfolded the plan of salvation and His mission to the world. In none of His subsequent discourses did He explain so fully, step by step, the work necessary to be done in the hearts of all who would

God's Footprint on My Floor

inherit the kingdom of heaven" (Ellen G. White, *The Desire of Ages,* p. 176).

It was extremely difficult, however, for the strict Pharisee, who prided himself in his good works, to acknowledge his need of change. Being a cautious and thoughtful individual, Nicodemus pondered Jesus' words for a long time.

"Nicodemus hid the truth in his heart, and for three years there was little apparent fruit.

"But Jesus was acquainted with the soil into which He cast the seed. . . . For a time Nicodemus did not publicly acknowledge Christ, but he watched His life, and pondered His teachings. In the Sanhedrin council he repeatedly thwarted the schemes of the priests to destroy Him. When at last Jesus was lifted up on the cross, Nicodemus remembered the teaching upon Olivet: 'As Moses lifted up the serpent in the wilderness, even so must the Son of man be lifted up: that whosoever believeth in Him should not perish, but have eternal life.' The light from that secret interview illumined the cross upon Calvary, and Nicodemus saw in Jesus the world's Redeemer.

"After the Lord's ascension, when the disciples were scattered by persecution, Nicodemus came boldly to the front. He employed his wealth in sustaining the infant church that the Jews had expected to be blotted out at the death of Christ. In the time of peril he who had been so cautious and questioning was firm as a rock, encouraging the faith of the disciples, and furnishing means to carry forward the work of the gospel. He was scorned and persecuted by those who had paid

1951

Give Your Guilt Away

him reverence in other days. He became poor in this world's goods; yet he faltered not in the faith which had its beginning in that night conference with Jesus" (ibid., 176, 177).

Before the proud Pharisee could give his guilt away and accept the new life Christ longed to bestow on him, he had to recognize his need, admit his guilt and sin, and turn to Christ, who alone could take away that guilt and sin. When he saw Christ dying on the cross in his stead, Nicodemus' heart broke, and he fully accepted his dying Saviour.

When we, too, recognize our need, when we become convinced of our guilt, just how do we find the forgiveness that Christ longs to give? King David wanted his neighbor's wife, Bathsheba, so he had her husband, an army man, placed at the most dangerous point when his outfit went into battle. As David had planned, Uriah was killed. When David took Bathsheba for his own wife, the Lord sent the prophet Nathan to point out his sin. David recognized his wrong and offered a beautiful prayer of repentance: "Have mercy upon me, O God, according to thy lovingkindness: according unto the multitude of thy tender mercies blot out my transgressions. Wash me throughly from mine iniquity, and cleanse me from my sin. For I acknowledge my transgressions: and my sin is ever before me. Against thee, thee only, have I sinned, and done this evil in thy sight" (Psalm 51:1-4).

David expressed his faith in God's willingness and ability to forgive in verse 7: "Purge me with hyssop, and I shall be clean: wash me, and I shall

God's Footprint on My Floor

be whiter than snow." And his final plea demonstrates just how God will answer such prayers. "Create in me a clean heart, O God; and renew a right spirit within me" (verse 10). David gave his guilt away and found God's pardon.

Every plea for forgiveness should contain the two elements evidenced in David's prayer. First, we need cleansing from our sin. Second, we need to accept a new and right spirit that will help us in the future to follow God's will and desire for us.

If we still feel guilty about the past and are ashamed to face up to our weaknesses and sins, we need to come humbly before God, open the Bible to Psalm 51, and read aloud the first ten verses. Then we can say to God, "This is the way I feel. Please do create in me—right now—a clean heart and renew a right spirit within me." God answered David's prayer in spite of the enormity of his crime, and He'll do so for each of us, no matter what we've done. It's the only way we can give our guilt away.

God specifically promises in 1 John 1:9, "If we confess our sins, he is faithful and just to forgive us our sins, and to cleanse us from *all* unrighteousness." The only *if* is "if we confess"; the rest is sure. God promises to cleanse us from *all* unrighteousness and He doesn't lie. However, we're likely to lie, especially to ourselves. We don't like to admit that we're guilty sinners before God and our fellowman. Because He knows how hard it is for us to recognize our need, God plainly tells us, "If we say that we have not sinned, we make him a liar, and his word is not in us" (1 John 1:10).

Give Your Guilt Away

Our confession, though, must not come just from a sense of shame. It must come from the Holy Spirit's influence in our lives. It should be the outpouring of our inmost soul in appreciation of Jesus, who died for our sins so that we might find forgiveness and eternal life through Him. God wants you to know how much He loves you. When you do wrong He's not angry with you but grieves to see you hurting yourself.

We should also be aware that God cannot accept our confession unless we're sincere, unless we have allowed Him to genuinely reform our lives. We don't have to be perfect before we repent and confess our sins, but the purifying work of the Holy Spirit will mark our sincerity and will bring the breath of life and the peace of God to our lives.

Once God has forgiven us, we must learn to forgive ourselves and not worry about that which we've done in the past. No matter what we've done, when we pray, "Father, forgive me," He does just that. We then stand before Him as His sons and daughters, free from all sin because Jesus paid the price for every one of them.

At the age of seventeen John Newton was drafted into the British Navy and led a typical, reckless sailor's life. He was not only immoral but also a troublemaker. Once he was publicly whipped for trying to desert. Newton later captained a ship engaged in the slave trade. One night in a terrible storm that threatened apparent death he prayed for the first time since he had been a boy, pledging to quit the slave trade and give his life to Christ.

God spared John Newton's life, and he later

studied for the ministry and was ordained as a deacon in 1764. Newton's conversion was so dramatic and his preaching so intense that crowds flocked to hear his dynamic witness. In addition, he composed 281 gospel hymns; but the one which above all others expresses Newton's intense sorrow for his sins and his willingness to give them to Christ is:

> "Amazing grace! how sweet the sound
> That saved a wretch like me!
> I once was lost, but now am found;
> Was blind, but now I see.
>
> " 'Twas grace that taught my heart to fear,
> And grace my fears relieved;
> How precious did that grace appear,
> The hour I first believed!
>
> "Through many dangers, toils, and snares,
> I have already come;
> 'Tis grace hath brought me safe thus far,
> And grace will lead me home."

That same amazing grace makes it possible for you to give your guilt away. It's quite an exchange. Christ takes our lives of sin and guilt and gives us instead His sinless life and clean heart. Don't you want to avail yourself of a bargain like that? You'll never get a better one!

Give Your Guilt Away

CHRIST'S ANSWER TO MAN'S NEED

(Based on the Beatitudes in Matthew 5)

OUR PROBLEM	CHRIST'S ANSWER	RESULTS
1. PRIDE INSECURITY POOR SELF-IMAGE	(Blessed are . . .) * THE POOR IN SPIRIT Those who recognize their need and begin to do something about it	* Acceptance of self * Conquest of false pride * Meaningful communion with God and man
2. SIN AND GUILT	* THEY THAT MOURN Repentance for and turning from sin	* Clear conscience * Evidence of acceptance by God and man
3. REBELLIOUSNESS, ANGER, LACK OF CONFIDENCE	* THE MEEK Submissiveness and dedication to the will of God for us	* Acceptance of authority * Development of trust and confidence in God and man

How to Live in a Pressure Cooker

We live in the pressure cooker of a strongly competitive way of life, and these pressures are increasing steadily in spite of all the gadgets we have which are supposed to make life easier. In fact, some think our stress has increased proportionately to the development of our gadgets.

Storms that come upon us from outside, as well as the petty things that disturb us from within, violently affect our nervous systems. Although every part of the human body is affected to some extent by these disturbances, none registers our changing emotions as quickly as the stomach. The old philosopher's observation that "the stomach is the mirror of the mind" holds much truth. The peculiar ways our stomach reacts reveal our innermost thoughts and feelings.

"Some years ago a child swallowed some food so hot that it scalded his gullet and closed the tube to his stomach. Physicians made a new opening, and the child lived in spite of the inconvenience of having to be fed, not through his mouth, but through the new opening in his abdomen.

"Physicians saw this as an opportunity to study

stomach function by peering through this artificial opening. The child, now a grown man, serves as a laboratory worker and has been the subject of some very interesting experiments.

"One day the man became angry about something during an experiment, and immediately the doctors observed that the stomach became very active, pouring out large quantities of acid juices, even changing its color to a deep red corresponding to the flushed and red face the patient now had. In fact, so engorged did the little blood vessels of the stomach become that some of them actually burst, and little pin-point hemorrhages appeared.

"But that was not the only interesting effect. It was also noted that when the man was depressed, sad, or fearful, his mental state was again reflected in the stomach. There was less blood flow, less gastric juice, and the movement of the stomach was slower.

"Besides, let us point out that the sequence of these conditions, such as increased stomach acidity, the small hemorrhages in the stomach lining, and stomach activity, is the group of events that can lead the small hemorrhages to become eroded; and the high acid helps to eat out a small crater. This is one of the ways to develop ulcers of the stomach.

"When Tom—for that was the man's name—was happy and enjoying his work the stomach assumed its normal color, the blood flowing through it was normal, and the amount of gastric juice that was secreted was just right.

"This is indeed a remarkable experiment and

a scientific observation that supports the belief that the stomach is closely related to the mind and to the emotions" (J. Wayne McFarland, MD, *Better Living*, pp. 92, 93).

We have two kinds of muscles: the voluntary muscles, such as the muscles that move our arms and hands, which respond to our wishes; the involuntary muscles, such as the muscles that control our heartbeat, which function without our direct control. And it's a good thing that we have the involuntary muscle system. Otherwise it would take all our effort and concentration just to keep our heart beating and our lungs filled with air, and whenever we would have to add to that effort the work of digestion, things would get so complicated that we'd probably forget some vital function and die! But fortunately all these systems act automatically. However, they do respond to *thoughts that engender emotions.*

There are helpful or constructive emotions, and there are harmful or destructive emotions.

Helpful–Constructive	*Harmful–Destructive*
Love	Hate
Gratitude	Revenge
Sympathy	Anger
Courage	Fright
Joy	Despondency
Confidence	Envy
Contentment	Jealousy
Lead to HEALTH	Lead to SICKNESS

Why is it that the harmful, destructive emotions

often lead to physical problems and sickness? Pains arising from physical effort are usually no problem. We can stop what we are doing and wait till the pain is over. But emotional pains are different. We cannot turn off our emotions quite so easily. Because they are likely to remain with us all day and often most of the night as well, we tend to suffer far more from the results of nervous tension than we do from any mere physical effort. And continued stress and tension lead most certainly to sickness and ill health. Some of the medical problems that can be attributed to this cause are stomach and abdominal problems, chronic skin troubles, arthritis, tension headaches, nervous colitis, high blood pressure, mental disorders, increased smoking and consumption of alcohol which lead to physical damage.

These are not imaginary troubles. They are real physical disorders—even though nervous tensions may have caused them; so, harmful, destructive emotions often lead to serious medical problems.

When we come right down to it, we cannot have good health and good nerves without having good thoughts. We cannot have physical health and harbor thoughts of fear, hate, resentment, jealousy, selfishness, and worry. These produce tension which result in frustration, dissatisfaction, loneliness, and emptiness in the life.

When the pressure builds up too much, the natural reaction is to blow our lid. Anger is fundamentally a means of self-protection. The baby who becomes hungry expresses his need by manifesting his anger. We're supposed to learn, as we mature, to control our emotions in order to live success-fully. But emotions are powerful, and merely re-pressing them can cause physical damage. High blood pressure, ulcers, headaches, and other such physical symptoms can often result from poorly directed emotions.

Truly controlling our emotions consists of not suppressing them, but first of all learning to recog-nize them for what they are and then intelligently directing them into proper outlets. Giving vent to the right kind of emotions, as mentioned previ-ously, can be very helpful physically.

Therefore we must recognize some of our under-lying attitudes for what they are. One of our most destructive emotions is hatred, sometimes termed "misguided love." It is the same force as love, only it is misdirected and turned destructive. But even most Christians blind themselves to the fact that they have from time to time such negative emotions. However, anything we do that attempts to build up ourselves at the expense of others falls into this category. It's easy to excuse ourselves by saying, "Oh, that's righteous indignation . . . or justifiable anger . . . or normal resentment . . . or constructive criticism." But whatever name you call them, they are divisive and destructive and actually harm us more than they hurt others. For instance, the overly critical person who finds it difficult to forgive others suffers from a form of hate.

Hostility is the most destructive and most com-mon form of the emotional syndrome we're now discussing. The ideal, of course, is to become like Christ in this respect and never have any hostility at all, and God can do this for us. But we want to take one step at a time, and our emphasis at first is to cut down on the amount of hostility we feel.

Abraham Lincoln was probably one of the most bitterly attacked presidents in the history of our country. Following a particularly vicious attack on Lincoln, a distraught friend was amazed that he remained so calm through it all. To his inquiry Lincoln replied, "My feelings are unimportant. It's the country that counts." He had devoted his every energy and interest to the needs of his country —so much so that he could remain serene under intense personal attack. Christ, of course, offers the classic example when He allowed Himself to be accused, beaten, and spit upon without retaliation. Then as they drove the spikes into His hands, He prayed, "Father, forgive them; for they know not what they do."

When we free our interest and concentration from ourselves, a new day will begin as far as our own happiness is concerned and in our calm acceptance of all that befalls us in life. We'll neither respond hysterically or with hostility. We will have learned to live successfully, without blowing our lids, in this pressure cooker in which we find ourselves!

In order to have true calmness in our souls we must partake of the calmness and peace of heaven. Charles Kellogg, a noted naturalist, and a friend were walking together on Sixth Avenue in New York City amid all the noise, confusion, honking, and clanging of the great metropolis.

Suddenly Mr. Kellogg stopped and halted his

64

friend. "Listen," he said, "Do you hear that?"

"Hear what?"

"That cricket!"

The friend was amazed. "Cricket!" he exclaimed. "How could anybody hear the sound of a cricket with all this noise going on around us?"

"Come on, I'll show you," Kellogg replied. So saying, he led his friend down a basement stairway, and there in a niche of the wall sat a small black cricket singing its bedtime serenade to New York City.

"How could anyone have ears sharp enough to hear this cricket chirping in the midst of all this New York traffic?" his friend wondered.

"Come on, I'll show you," Kellogg said again. They went back up to the street level, and the naturalist took a coin out of his pocket and tossed it on the sidewalk. People all around stopped and looked toward the spot where the coin had fallen.

"You see," Kellogg explained, "the people have their ears tuned to money. I have mine tuned to the sounds of nature."

If God should speak to puzzled, bewildered, angry, and distraught modern man, what would be His first words? Psalm 46:10 has the answer, I believe: "Be still, and know that I am God." Psalm 46 has been designated Luther's Psalm because the great Reformer, who was accustomed to singing in time of trouble, paraphrased it in his hymn "A Mighty Fortress." The psalm is a glorious song on the theme that in the midst of the upheavals of nations, God's people are safe. Here amid the thunder of world crisis and catastrophe, God reminds His people to "be still, and know that I am God."

Our omnipotent God graciously invites us to cease our helter-skelter hustle and bustle and to take time to commune with Him. To the invitation "Be still," God adds, "and know that I am God." If these be the words of God, they place Him under a simple test by every sincere person, and He certainly will not disappoint anyone who follows the admonition. God longs for us to know Him, and if we follow His advice to "be still, and know that I am God," He will not disappoint us. But never before has it been so hard for men to listen. We are so deluged by shocks to our emotional system that we never seem to have time to recover from one blow until the next falls.

One day, the story goes, an earthly visitor appeared at the gate of heaven. Asked the attending angel, "How did you enjoy God's beautiful world during your days on earth?"

The man replied, "Well, I didn't get a chance to see much of it. I was too busy telephoning and everything."

Alongside the roaring freeway of life on which civilization is rolling at ever-increasing speed stands man's Best Friend, God. To every traveler rushing by He urges, "Be still, and know that I am God."

Perhaps the glory and goodness of God is nowhere else so beautifully expressed as in the Book of Job. Job was sick from the soles of his feet to the top of his head, and during his illness he had visits from four of his friends: Eliphaz, Bildad, Zophar,

How to Live in a Pressure Cooker

and Elihu. They were all prominent citizens in their day and fell into a long, bitter argument with Job over the meaning of the trouble that had befallen him and over the question of God's dealings with men.

Job contended that because he had been a just and kind man, God was unfair and unjust in allowing the terrible sickness to come upon him. Job believed that God was no longer willing to listen to his prayers, and he even pleaded for an opportunity to speak with God: "Then Job answered and said, Even to day is my complaint bitter: my stroke is heavier than my groaning. Oh that I knew where I might find him! that I might come even to his seat! I would order my cause before him, and fill my mouth with arguments. I would know the words which he would answer me, and understand what he would say unto me" (Job 23:1-5).

Somehow Job seemed to think that God was hiding from him. "Behold, I go forward," he declared, "but he is not there; and backward, but I cannot perceive him: on the left hand, where he doth work, but I cannot behold him: he hideth himself on the right hand, that I cannot see him" (Job 23:8, 9).

Although Job seemed to think that he was ready to debate with God, his faith still clung to Him, for he tells us: "But he knoweth the way that I take: when he hath tried me, I shall come forth as gold" (Job 23:10).

Job thought that God had dealt unfairly with him and that even if he could face Him, God would not be able to answer his arguments.

God's Footprint on My Floor

His friends who had come to comfort him were not very helpful. They seemed to be saying, "Why, Job, the fact that you are sick is the evidence that you have sinned against God. If He doesn't listen to you, it is because you are such a sinful man." In fact, they told him in chapter 11, verse 6: "Know therefore that God exacteth of thee less than thine iniquity deserveth." They continued their counsel in chapter 22, verse 5, with these words: "Is not thy wickedness great? and thine iniquities infinite?"

This sort of talk angered Job, for he viewed himself as a very righteous man. He couldn't think of any sin that would have caused all of his trouble. "No doubt but ye are the people, and wisdom shall die with you. But I have understanding as well as you; I am not inferior to you: yea, who knoweth not such things as these?" (Job 12:2, 3). And later he added, "I have heard many such things: miserable comforters are ye all" (Job 16:2).

Now all these men were mistaken, Job as well as his friends. They had talked so much about God that they did not give God a chance to tell them about Himself. Finally, after they had run out of words, God revealed Himself to them. Particularly addressing His remarks to Job, He begins, "Who is this that darkeneth counsel by words without knowledge?" (Job 38:2). In the following verses God challenges: "Gird up now thy loins like a man; for I will demand of thee, and answer thou me. Where wast thou when I laid the foundations of the earth? declare, if thou hast understanding" (Job 38:3, 4).

Don't you think that God is saying the same

thing to many today who think they know even more than God? I see God today answering them in the same way. "Who is this that darkeneth counsel by words without knowledge?" "Where were you when I laid the foundations of the earth? If you know so much, tell us all about it."

God then spoke to Job from the book of nature. He told him about Creation and earth and air and sky, about day and night and thunder and lightning. He pointed to the stars and the clouds. He told Job about many of the animals that demonstrate man's feebleness in comparison to the great and almighty power of the Creator.

As God paused a moment, Job answered, "Behold, I am vile; what shall I answer thee? I will lay mine hand upon my mouth" (40:4). And apparently he proceeded to do just that, because we find God speaking to him again, telling about some of the additional wonders in nature, about the great beasts that He had created and the instincts He had given them. Job, overwhelmed by it all, finally confessed: "I know that thou canst do every thing, and that no thought can be withholden from thee. . . . Therefore have I uttered that I understood not; things too wonderful for me, which I knew not. . . . I have heard of thee by the hearing of the ear: but now mine eye seeth thee" (Job 42:2, 3, 5).

When Job and his friends stopped arguing and finally decided to be still for a little while, God was able to begin to reveal Himself. When his restless soul was stilled and he opened his mind to God, Job really came to know his Creator.

Lots of our hostility, fear, and frustration in life

God's Footprint on My Floor

come from not understanding what life is all about and from not trusting God to know what is best for us. When Job came to this understanding, he overcame his hostility and prayed for his friends. The Scripture records, "And the Lord turned the captivity of Job, when he prayed for his friends: also the Lord gave Job twice as much as he had before" (Job 42:10).

God challenges us, "Be still, and know that I am God. Still your words. Silence your prejudices and your preconceived opinions. Quiet the clamor of your pride and selfishness. Come to Me, trust in Me, and things will be pleasanter and better and happier for you than ever before. Forget your competitiveness. Pray for those who misunderstand and abuse you."

All this is what Jesus pronounced in the Beatitude on which we are focusing as the next step in God's answers to man's problems, and yet it is probably misunderstood more than any of the other Beatitudes. Matthew 5:5 puts it this way: "Blessed are the meek: for they shall inherit the earth."

A group of college students in Japan once told me they thought Christianity was a cowardly sort of religion because it emphasizes meekness. I did my best to explain that the meekness which Jesus commends describes the quiet submission to the life of God. Such commitment is based on our confidence that He will provide all that is best for us. It involves victory over our clamoring selfishness. It marks our deliverance from the tyranny of the stresses of the hectic lives we now lead.

Yet it's not easy to be meek in the Christian

How to Live in a Pressure Cooker

sense. Actually it's the most difficult struggle in the world, for true submission involves emptying ourselves as fully as Christ did for us. In order to help us achieve this ideal God has given two laws of life designed to help us develop healthy mental and emotional attitudes.

The first is—*we are what we choose to be.* The wisdom which God gave to the ancient Hebrews appears in the proverb which states, "As he thinketh in his heart, so is he" (Proverbs 23:7). Linus, a cartoon character, charged with breaking a lamp and told he had no one to blame it on but himself, pondered, then ventured, "Maybe I could blame it on society!"

We often overlook the power of the *will.* Rightly directed, the will can actually impart energy to the whole being and help maintain health. Dr. Norman Vincent Peale has helped a lot of people, and has made a fortune too, through advocating "the power of positive thinking."

The Chicago *Tribune,* under the headline "Health as a Matter of Choice," reported that in New York state in 1968 lower, very encouraging death rates were reported in certain diseases, but in three areas there were higher death rates. These were deaths from motor-vehicle accidents, lung cancer, and cirrhosis of the liver. In commentary on this a news note stated:

"It's worth noting that incidence of these last three has been correlated with *voluntary* actions: irresponsible driving causes many motor-vehicle accidents; heavy smoking increases danger of lung cancer; intemperate drinking leads to cirrhosis.

God's Footprint on My Floor

What Dr. Ingraham's report suggests is that good health and long life are becoming less and less functions of luck or chance, and more and more fruits of sensible habits" (*Reader's Digest*, August, 1969, p. 12).

The second law we can use to meet the special problems of living in our world of rapid change is—*thoughts and feelings are encouraged and strengthened as we give them expression.* The author of the book *The Ministry of Healing* lists the following as "health's greatest safeguard": gratitude, rejoicing, benevolence, [and] trust" (p. 281). Just a little time and effort will develop these safeguards, and they will strengthen as we express them.

1. *Gratitude.* Hans Selye, famous researcher in the field of stress at the University of Montreal in Quebec, states, "It seems to me that, among all the emotions, there is one which, *more than any other,* accounts for the absence or presence of stress in human relations: the feeling of gratitude, with its negative counterpart, the need for revenge" (*The Stress of Life*, p. 284, emphasis supplied). Yet how seldom we seem to hear the pleasant expression Thank you, and how even more rare it is to receive a thank-you note.

2. *Rejoicing.* Another of the ancient Hebrew proverbs states, "A merry heart doeth good like a medicine" (Proverbs 17:22).

3. *Benevolence.* We're talking now about the old Boy Scout idea—a good deed every day. We improve our own health as well as help others when we practice simple, everyday kindnesses.

How to Live in a Pressure Cooker

72

If each of us would be just a little more thoughtful each day to those in the home, to those with whom we labor, and to those we meet, how much easier it would be to live in our stressful age! And many of the little courtesies we might manifest are like the smile the poet wrote about—worth a million dollars, but costing not a penny.

4. *Trust.* One of the major problems Americans seem to have today is that of trusting people. Our disillusionment with both philosophies and politicians in recent years has helped bring this about. However, it's necessary to trust our fellowman even though sometimes we may be disappointed. But even more helpful in meeting those problems that seem beyond human ability to cope with is the ability to trust and confide in the Friend who is more than human.

We want to utilize everything that can possibly help us meet the complexities of living in the "man on the moon age." We have conquered space, but a myriad of complex problems remain unsolved here on Earth—problems that every day affect our health and happiness.

This is the age of open-mindedness—men are searching anywhere and everywhere for answers. Medical researchers today are even willing to consider household remedies and witch doctor's techniques to see if they can find something that may help overcome some of our baffling medical problems.

But there is another often-neglected course that thinking men and women are beginning to turn to as they meet the seemingly insuperable problems

God's Footprint on My Floor

and tensions of modern life—trust in divine power. When we put our trust in the power of our Creator, it will help us untangle the knots in our lives and in our stomachs. We will find peace of mind and body that will enable us to live more useful, meaningful, and happy lives. As we share this experience with others, we'll become part of the solution to man's overtaxed mind.

Because He loves us so much, because He wants us to enjoy the best of life here, because He has eternal plans for those who are becoming His sons and daughters, our loving Saviour invites us as He did those on the mountainside so long ago: "Come unto me, all ye that labour and are heavy laden." If we will lay aside the clamor of this world and cast all our cares on the One who cares for us, we will hear His quiet voice of confident love promising, "Come—and I will give you peace."

How to Live in a Pressure Cooker

CHRIST'S ANSWER TO MAN'S NEED

(Based on the Beatitudes in Matthew 5)

OUR PROBLEM	CHRIST'S ANSWER	RESULTS
1. PRIDE INSECURITY POOR SELF-IMAGE	(Blessed are . . .) * THE POOR IN SPIRIT Those who recognize their need and begin to do something about it	* Acceptance of self * Conquest of false pride * Meaningful communion with God and man
2. SIN AND GUILT	* THEY THAT MOURN Repentance for and turning from sin	* Clear conscience * Evidence of acceptance by God and man
3. REBELLIOUSNESS, ANGER, LACK OF CONFIDENCE	* THE MEEK Submissiveness and dedication to the will of God for us	* Acceptance of authority * Development of trust and confidence in God and man
4. UNHAPPINESS, FEAR, FRUSTRATION, WORRY	* THEY WHICH DO HUNGER AND THIRST AFTER RIGHTEOUS-NESS Filled with the Water of life—justification	* Healthy emotions * Wholistic development * Right with God and man

Chapter 6

"Materiosclerosis" —the World's Greatest Killer

Many in our world today are turning to materialism or drugs or other escape mechanisms in an endless search for more and more of that which does not satisfy. They spend their time in living it up but not really finding life at its best. They are so dominated by the tyranny of things that they hold garage sales to get rid of things they don't know what to do with so that they may have more room for new things which they will quickly not know what to do with either.

A certain man had a wife with a desperate desire for things. She was always pestering him to get something for her—a new coat, a new car, pearls, furs, baubles without end. Since her husband was a top businessman, he could gratify her every wish. He also bought burial plots for both himself and his wife against the eventual day of their passing, selected the tombstones, and ordered the inscriptions. "On my wife's," he instructed the engraver, "put, 'She Died of Things.' And on mine write, 'He Died Providing Them for Her.' "

The great American rat race seems to consist of trampling everyone else in order to get more "superduper, electromagic, self-defrosting, miracle-tuning, and marvel-making gadgets and contraptions to take the place, for a small down payment, of last year's models of the very same things." And the result? Arteriosclerosis, hypertension, and coronary heart disease. But actually, arteriosclerosis is not the killer. It should really be "materiosclerosis," for we're dying from the highly competitive effort to accumulate things. Cardiovascular diseases may kill their hundreds of thousands each year, but materiosclerosis kills millions.

There's a better way, a happier way, a way to live it up and still enjoy life at its best. God has something better for us—something better than we ever thought we might possibly have.

One day Jesus—hungry, tired, and thirsty—stood by the well outside the Samaritan village of Sychar. The disciples had gone into town to get something to drink, and as a Samaritan woman was about to draw water, He asked for a drink. In the conversation which ensued He didn't disparage Jacob's well or the water in it, for she would have considered that pure chauvinism. Instead Jesus offered her something better. "If thou knewest the gift of God," He told her, "and who it is that saith to thee, Give me to drink; thou wouldest have asked of him, and he would have given thee living water" (John 4:10).

The Bible uses water to symbolize man's cleansing from sin by Christ, the true Water of life. God used water at the time of Noah's flood to purify the world from sin. The Hebrew sanctuary contained a laver of water where the priest washed

"Materiosclerosis"—the World's Greatest Killer

the sacrifices and himself—a symbol of purification from sin. Baptism by immersion and the foot-washing service instituted by Christ at the Lord's Supper have become Christian symbols of washing away the filth of sin.

And this brings us to the fourth Beatitude: "Blessed are they which do hunger and thirst after righteousness: for they shall be filled." Jesus here refers to water as that righteousness which becomes ours when we are cleansed by His grace. This righteousness is so essential to the Christian life that if one doesn't have it, he is pictured as a desperate person crawling across the desolate desert in search of something to quench the agony of his parched throat.

The quest for happiness is really the soul's desire for righteousness. Most of us sense an emptiness in life and have a craving for that which will satisfy, but we often don't even know how to identify that for which we are restlessly, endlessly searching. We do know, however, that when we gain the material things which are considered the rewards of ambition, they don't really satisfy. "No human agent can supply that which will satisfy the hunger and thirst of the soul" (Ellen White, *Thoughts From the Mount of Blessing*, p. 18).

We have a thirst which only the Water of life can satisfy. Now the righteousness of God is embodied in Christ, for His life was the only demonstration of genuine righteousness since the inception of sin. We receive righteousness only by receiving Him, and He will freely give it to everyone who hungers and thirsts to receive it.

God's Footprint on My Floor

I am reminded of Isaiah 41:17, 18: "When the poor and needy seek water, and there is none, and their tongue faileth for thirst, I the Lord will hear them, I the God of Israel will not forsake them. I will open rivers in high places, and fountains in the midst of the valleys: I will make the wilderness a pool of water, and the dry land springs of water." Christ is the fountain of pure water freely given to make us righteous in God's sight.

The fourth Beatitude uses also another figure of speech: not only does Jesus speak of *thirsting* for righteousness but also of *hungering* for it. The Scriptures use bread to represent our daily dependence on Christ for the development and growth of righteousness. Bread aptly illustrates both physical and spiritual need and points us to God's purposes. From the shewbread of the sanctuary to the Communion bread which Paul mentions in 1 Corinthians 11—all show God's loving provision for the salvation and restoration of humanity.

The hunger we have for our daily bread and the craving we call thirst fittingly represent our need for the essentials of spiritual life: water, representing Christ's justifying power, which cleanses us from sin; and bread, representing His sanctifying power, which brings us daily growth in righteousness.

Isaiah used a similar metaphor in one of the Bible's most interesting challenges: "Ho, every one that thirsteth, come ye to the waters, and he that hath no money; come ye, buy, and eat. . . . Wherefore do ye spend money for that which is not bread? and your labour for that which satisfieth not? hearken diligently unto me, and eat ye that

"Materiosclerosis"—the World's Greatest Killer

which is good. . . . Incline your ear, and come unto me: hear, and your soul shall live" (Isaiah 55:1-3).

We often spend money for that which is not bread, buying and laboring for those things which do not bring health either to the body or the soul. "Why?" Isaiah asks. "Diligently hearken unto me," our Lord invites. "Come unto me, . . . and your soul shall live."

Did you notice Isaiah's strange proposition? "Ho, every one that thirsteth," he wrote, "come ye to the waters, and he that hath no money; come ye, buy, and eat." How can we buy without money? We go back to an earlier Beatitude for our answer. "Blessed are the poor in spirit." Isaiah is talking about those who have no money spiritually. They not only recognize their need, but also that they have no merits to offer God as payment for salvation. God invites us to come in spite of our spiritual poverty. All we have to bring is our empty cup.

But we must hunger for the Bread of life and thirst for the Water of life. We must put forth every effort to secure them. Salvation is free, but discipleship costs all we have to give. God has never promised to bestow salvation upon anyone who is unwilling to put forth the effort to obtain it.

A little boy peered into the window of a candy store back in the days when a penny gave him a choice of several delectable treats. His mother, impatiently waiting for him to make up his mind, urged, "Come on, Timmy. Make up your mind. We have to hurry along."

"But, Mommy," he replied, "I only have one penny to spend."

God's Footprint on My Floor

You and I have only one life to spend. Let's spend it right by putting our time, interest, and effort into the greatest bargain of them all. Salvation through Christ is ours without money or price, because the price was so high that only He could pay it for us. Now it is ours for the asking for all who hunger and thirst. "Incline your ear," cries the Heavenly Merchantman. "Come unto me: hear, and your soul shall live."

"Materiosclerosis"—the World's Greatest Killer

CHRIST'S ANSWER TO MAN'S NEED
(Based on the Beatitudes in Matthew 5)

OUR PROBLEM	CHRIST'S ANSWER	RESULTS
1. PRIDE INSECURITY POOR SELF-IMAGE	(Blessed are . . .) * THE POOR IN SPIRIT Those who recognize their need and begin to do something about it	*Acceptance of self *Conquest of false pride *Meaningful communion with God and man
2. SIN AND GUILT	* THEY THAT MOURN Repentance for and turning from sin	*Clear conscience *Evidence of acceptance by God and man
3. REBELLIOUSNESS, ANGER, LACK OF CONFIDENCE	* THE MEEK Submissiveness and dedication to the will of God for us	*Acceptance of authority *Development of trust and confidence in God and man
4. UNHAPPINESS, FEAR, FRUSTRATION, WORRY	* THEY WHICH DO HUNGER AND THIRST AFTER RIGHTEOUS-NESS Filled with the Water of life—justification	*Healthy emotions *Wholistic development *Right with God and man
5. BITTERNESS AND SELFISHNESS	* THE MERCIFUL Forgiving attitude, willingness to share, spiritual growth	*Improvement of relationships *Identification, sharing *Love to God and man

Chapter 7

"Going, Going, Gone"

If you've ever been to an auction, you're well acquainted with the auctioneer's chant: "Going, going, gone . . ." That's the title given to an article that appeared in *Christianity Today.*

"When the daily paper arrives, my wife hastens to cut out the auction advertisements and burn them. Otherwise I would attend the auctions—all of them. I have a mania for them, no matter what's being sold.

"One hot summer afternoon I found myself standing for two hours in the blazing sun at a bicycle auction. Nothing else there—just bicycles. That has to be considered a strange use of time for someone whose storage shed already housed four bikes.

"To justify my strange behavior I pointed out to my friends that auctions provide an interesting study in the values and tastes of the bidders as well as a glimpse into the lives of those who originally collected the junk—or treasure, as the case may be.

"I have pondered the generation gap while watching a Harley-Davidson motorcycle and a Queene Anne chair being auctioned as part of the same estate.

84

"What schizophrenia of taste, I have wondered, could account for the fact that one house spawned both a reasonably good collection of original art and a vast collection of *Reader's Digest* condensed books?

"But the most interesting exercise at an auction is trying to deduce why people are willing to pay what they do for some of the stranger items. What inner longing is satisfied by the acquisition of an item that is totally useless or consummately ugly?

"At one sale the auctioneer held up an intricately contrived device incorporating two cog wheels, three prongs, a spring, and a lever arm. It was the kind of thing my teenager would call a 'do golly.'

"When the auctioneer called for a starting offer, one cautious bidder asked, 'What is it?' The auctioneer examined the device with a puzzled look and replied, 'I don't know, but if you've got another one this one would make it a pair.'

"Everyone laughed, but someone bought it.

"At another sale I watched with fascination as two sixtyish women claimed their purchases: two Mae West shaped vases garishly decorated with blue-green vines. They were aglow with their triumph in being the successful bidders on the twin monstrosities.

"I have observed perfectly sane people bidding more than the current retail price for items that had been badly used.

"Over and over again as I've attended auctions I've found myself saying, 'They paid *that* for *those?*' I'm sure some of those people have later said the same thing to themselves.

"Going, Going, Gone"

"I wonder if some dweller in a far-off planet looks at God's redemptive transaction on earth and thinks of His choices, 'He paid *that* for *those*?'

"But as Publilius Syrus pointed out, 'Everything is worth what its purchaser will pay for it' " ("Eutychus and His Kin," October 8, 1971, p. 34).

Although it's hard to believe, Christ paid far more for us than we seem to be worth! But on the other hand, maybe we undervalue ourselves. "Everything is worth what its purchaser will pay for it." Obviously we are worth a fantastic price to Him. He gave all He had for us. Why? Because He loves us. "God so loved the world, that he *gave*. . . ." It is the nature of love to give.

Christ not only gave His all for us but *emptied* Himself for us, according to Philippians 2:5-8. And we should share in this same kind of willingness to give. "Have this mind among yourselves, which you have in Christ Jesus, who, though he was in the form of God, did not count equality with God a thing to be grasped, but emptied himself, taking the form of a servant, being born in the likeness of men. And being found in human form he humbled himself and became obedient unto death, even death on a cross" (RSV).

Notice Christ's successive steps in emptying Himself:

1. He didn't think that equality with God was more important than identifying Himself with us so that He could become our Saviour.
2. He "emptied himself, taking the form of a servant." He who had been the Lord of the universe now became subservient to God.

God's Footprint on My Floor

3. Not only did He assume a subservient form, but He took the form of humanity, which means, according to Hebrews 2:7, that He became lower than even the angels.
4. But His emptying didn't stop there. Next we are told that He became mortal—"obedient unto death."
5. There is still one more step in Christ's emptying of self. The death He chose was the worst kind of all: the shameful, humiliating execution reserved for the vilest of criminals in the Roman Empire—"death on a cross."

Jesus could do no more. He emptied Himself fully and completely. In His glorious example, however, we see the results of His willingness to lay self completely aside, for the record in Philippians 2:9, 10 continues, "Therefore God has highly exalted him and bestowed on him the name which is above every name, that at the name of Jesus every knee should bow, in heaven and on earth and under the earth" (RSV). By giving all, Jesus was highly exalted to the place where every knee in the universe will bow to His supreme authority. Humble and unselfish love gives all, but as it gives it gains. The book *The Desire of Ages* puts it this way: "There is nothing, save the selfish heart of man, that lives unto itself. No bird that cleaves the air, no animal that moves upon the ground, but ministers to some other life. There is no leaf of the forest, or lowly blade of grass, but has its ministry. Every tree and shrub and leaf pours forth that element of life without which neither man nor animal could live; and man and animal, in turn, minister to the life of tree and shrub and leaf. The flowers breathe fragrance and unfold their beauty in blessing to the world. The sun sheds its light to gladden a thousand worlds. The ocean, itself the source of all our springs and fountains, receives the streams from every land, but takes to give. The mists ascending from its bosom fall in showers to water the earth, that it may bring forth and bud. . . .

"But turning from all lesser representations, we behold God in Jesus. Looking unto Jesus we see that it is the glory of our God to give. 'I do nothing of Myself,' said Christ; 'the living Father hath sent Me, and I live by the Father.' 'I seek not Mine own glory,' but the glory of Him that sent Me. John 8:28; 6:57; 8:50; 7:18. In these words is set forth the great principle which is the law of life for the universe. All things Christ received from God, but He took to give. So in the heavenly courts, in His ministry for all created beings: through the beloved Son, the Father's life flows out to all; through the Son it returns, in praise and joyous service, a tide of love, to the great Source of all. And thus through Christ the circuit of beneficence is complete, representing the character of the great Giver, the law of life" (pages 20, 21).

But another law operates in our sinful world. The paragraphs just quoted from *The Desire of Ages* begin with these words: "There is nothing, save the selfish heart of man, that lives unto itself." The world today is incurably sick. It's suffering from a disease that you don't hear mentioned on the radio or don't read about in the papers. Even the medical profession for the most part chooses to

God's Footprint on My Floor

ignore it, although its victims number in the tens of millions and are found in every country of the world.

The two chief symptoms of this disease are "ingrowing eyeballs" and "itching palms." Itching palms, of course, are always on the grab, and ingrowing eyeballs always make man see himself first.

By now you can identify the disease. It doesn't have a long scientific name. It's just plain old selfishness, the greatest epidemic of all time. It involves a subtle, all-permeating philosophy that causes men to engage in a restless, endless search for that which can never really satisfy. The Word of God sets this foolish quest before us in all its ridiculous madness by the penetrating query of Matthew 16:26: "What is a man profited, if he shall gain the whole world, and lose his own soul?"

We are dealing here with the law of life for the universe—to place God and others before ourselves. As we live for others and share with them, we actually grow in grace. As we give we gain. This is true not only physically but spiritually. Spiritual growth, or sanctification, necessitates constant exercise of the spiritual nature just as physical growth involves physical exercise. Such spiritual activity involves sharing Christ's mercies with those about us who have not yet received them. The growing, sanctified believer is a witness for the Lord Jesus Christ. Only as we give do we live. Notice how Jesus presents this experience as He develops the steps in Christian growth in the Beatitudes.

"Going, Going, Gone"

The fifth Beatitude recorded in Matthew 5:7 reads, "Blessed are the merciful: for they shall obtain mercy." Our hearts are by nature cold, selfish, and unloving. Only as we become God's children do we really overcome selfishness so that we can love our fellowmen in such a way that we share the mercies and blessings God gives us. As 1 John 4:19 tells us, "We love, because he first loved us" (RSV).

"The merciful are 'partakers of the divine nature,' and in them the compassionate love of God finds expression. All whose hearts are in sympathy with the heart of Infinite Love will seek to reclaim and not to condemn. Christ dwelling in the soul is a spring that never runs dry. Where He abides there will be an overflowing of beneficence.

"To the appeal of the erring, the tempted, the wretched victims of want and sin, the Christian does not ask, Are they worthy? but, How can I benefit them? In the most wretched, the most debased, he sees souls whom Christ died to save and for whom God has given to His children the ministry of reconciliation" (*Thoughts From the Mount of Blessing*, p. 22).

The Christian does not love or give *in order* to live. He gives and shares *because* he has new life in Christ. Our giving becomes the natural out-flowing of His love in our lives, and as we give we grow in grace.

The Christian's motivation for sharing is not that of obligation. Neither does he give because he's afraid not to, nor does he sacrifice to appease God. The Christian is not motivated to give by a desire to impress others with his generosity, or

God's Footprint on My Floor

for sake of earthly reward, or even in response to some emotional appeal. He gives because the love of God fills his life.

Paul tells us in 2 Corinthians 9:7, "God loveth a cheerful giver." The Greek word translated "cheerful" also lies behind our word *hilarious*. God loves one who is exhilarated by giving.

God Himself thrills in giving. As we discussed in the introduction to this chapter, Jesus *emptied* Himself for us without holding back, without calculating what He would get out of it, without measuring our worthiness. He gave freely, fully, and joyfully.

This same kind of mercy, love, and sharing —Jesus' kind—is to be the distinguishing mark of those who are becoming God's children.

"There are many to whom life is a painful struggle; they feel their deficiencies and are miserable and unbelieving; they think they have nothing for which to be grateful. Kind words, looks of sympathy, expressions of appreciation, would be to many a struggling and lonely one as the cup of cold water to a thirsty soul. A word of sympathy, an act of kindness, would lift burdens that rest heavily upon weary shoulders. And every word or deed of unselfish kindness is an expression of the love of Christ for lost humanity" (*ibid.*, p. 23).

Jerome K. Jerome in *The Passing of the Third Floor Back* tells of a mysterious stranger who moved into a shabby boardinghouse on Bloomsbury Place in London. The guests were bitter, quarrelsome, and self-centered, but the plain, gentle, and rather old-fashioned young man with

Christlike insight saw beneath each exterior the person who could and should exist there.

As he spoke with respectful kindness to the spinster of forty, who assumed that her bleached blonde hair and heavy makeup gave her the air of a coy twenty-one, she suddenly saw herself as a cheerful, bright-eyed woman coming toward middle age, but intelligent and interesting. Instantly she rejected the new image and snapped crossly at the young stranger. A few days later, though, she began to accept the new image, and her old self disappeared, to be seen no more.

An older boarder alienated the other guests by continually boasting of her wealthy and noble relatives. Subtly the stranger hinted that her own manners and appearance better indicated breeding than her words. In surprise she whispered to herself, "How foolish of me! People whose opinion is worth troubling about judge you by what you are, not by what you go about saying you are."

So it went on, with one after another changing into the person the young stranger seemed to see. When one foggy day the young man finally walked out of the boardinghouse and out of all their lives, he left behind people far different from those he had found in the beginning. Keen insight, gently imparted with concern and affection for even the least lovable of people, had wrought the transformation.

The results are just as dramatic for the one sharing, too, although this should not motivate our deeds of love and mercy. You'll remember that in the Beatitudes Jesus added to the blessing on the merciful this promise; "They shall obtain mercy." As we give we gain. We don't lose a thing when we share our blessings with those about us. "He who has given his life to God in ministry to His children is linked with Him who has all the resources of the universe at His command. His life is bound up by the golden chain of the immutable promises with the life of God. The Lord will not fail him in the hour of suffering and need. 'My God shall supply all your need according to His riches in glory by Christ Jesus.' Philippians 4:19. And in the hour of final need the merciful shall find refuge in the mercy of the compassionate Saviour and shall be received into everlasting habitations" (*Thoughts From the Mount of Blessing*, p. 24).

It isn't natural for us to give gladly and without reservation, because we are by nature selfish beings. But God invites us to become His children and to practice the law of life for the universe by letting His love so fill our lives that it will flow out to others.

Long ago in London a famous preacher had to deliver his sermons on the streets because the churches wouldn't allow him to speak inside. However, although people flocked to hear him preach, he wasn't reaching anyone in the upper classes.

One day while he was preaching, he saw his chance when a beautiful, well-cared-for carriage approached. He interrupted his sermon and asked the men near him who owned the splendid carriage. They replied that it belonged to Lady Ann Erskine, a social butterfly noted for her squandering of her husband's wealth on dress and parties. As Lady

"Going, Going, Gone"

Ann's carriage approached, the minister prayed that the Lord would help him reach her heart. When she came within earshot, he began to auction Lady Ann Erskine's soul. Quickly he recognized a bidder and called out, "Here's a bidder over here. It's Satan. Satan, what do you bid for the soul of Lady Ann Erskine?"

Satan replied, "All the wealth of the world, fine clothes, fine company, gaiety, and pleasures of all sorts."

"All right, then, Satan, what about after this life is ended? What do you offer then?" He waited —there was nothing but silence.

"Oh, here's another bidder. It's Jesus. Jesus, what do You offer for the soul of Lady Ann Erskine?"

"I offer a life of service for others—a cross of self-denial to carry in this life—but it brings real happiness to those willing to bear it. Then I offer eternal life in the kingdom I'm preparing for those who love and serve Me—eternal happiness amid all the splendors and pleasures of heaven."

The preacher's daring message strangely moved Lady Ann Erskine in her carriage, and she took but a moment to decide. Suddenly she stopped the carriage, stepped out, and walked over to the platform from which her soul had been put up for auction. Now realizing the hopeless condition of her self-seeking, she told the people gathered about her that she would gladly accept Christ's bid for her soul and dedicate her life to bearing His cross of service.

Lady Ann Erskine held true to her decision and

God's Footprint on My Floor

became known as the angel of the slums of London. She also wrote many inspiring Christian hymns.

The auction for our souls is not imaginary, and just two bidders—Christ and Satan—compete for our lives. Christ has already paid much for us, but we can still turn Him down and turn to Satan's offer of the baubles of pleasure and sin.

There are just two bidders, and you'll have to accept either the way of life, which is the way of unselfish love, or the way of death, which is to go on serving self. As you make your choice, remember these words of Christ. "Blessed are the merciful: for they shall obtain mercy." You are the auctioneer. You're making the choice right now. You're pronouncing the fateful words "Going, going . . ."

"Going, Going, Gone"

CHRIST'S ANSWER TO MAN'S NEED
(Based on the Beatitudes in Matthew 5)

OUR PROBLEM	CHRIST'S ANSWER	RESULTS
1. PRIDE INSECURITY POOR SELF-IMAGE	(Blessed are . . .) *THE POOR IN SPIRIT Those who recognize their need and begin to do something about it	*Acceptance of self *Conquest of false pride *Meaningful communion with God and man
2. SIN AND GUILT	*THEY THAT MOURN Repentance for and turning from sin	*Clear conscience *Evidence of acceptance by God and man
3. REBELLIOUSNESS, ANGER, LACK OF CONFIDENCE	*THE MEEK Submissiveness and dedication to the will of God for us	*Acceptance of authority *Development of trust and confidence in God and man
4. UNHAPPINESS, FEAR, FRUSTRATION, WORRY	*THEY WHICH DO HUNGER AND THIRST AFTER RIGHTEOUS-NESS Filled with the Water of life—justification	*Healthy emotions *Wholistic development *Right with God and man
5. BITTERNESS AND SELFISHNESS	*THE MERCIFUL Forgiving attitude, willingness to share, spiritual growth	*Improvement of relationships *Identification, sharing *Love to God and man
6. IMPURITY AND IMMORALITY	*THE PURE IN HEART Cleanliness, purity, integrity in life	*Moral freedom *Law of God in heart *Right doing toward God and man

Chapter 8

Calling a Spade a Steam Shovel

We live in a time when people aren't afraid to call a spade a *steam shovel*. It seems that we glory so much in our newfound freedom to "tell it like it is" that we often make what it is seem like something it isn't!

For instance, we hear a great deal about *love* today, but much of what we hear gives the wrong idea as to what love really is. We seem to have more discussion about love but also more strife and contention—not only overseas but right in our very homes. Maybe so much is being said that no one is even listening! Obviously it's time to stop and listen. What is love?

The citizens in the ancient city of Corinth literally prostituted love in the name of religion. The ancient temple on the Corinthian acropolis employed a thousand or more temple prostitutes. So, when the apostle Paul wrote to the Christians at Corinth, it was only natural that he define true love for them, which he does in 1 Corinthians 13.

In clarifying the meaning of love, Paul explained what it was not. First Corinthians tells us, first of all, that love is (1) not jealous, (2) not boastful, (3) not arrogant, (4) not rude, (5) not insistent on its own way, (6) not irritable, (7) not resentful, and (8) not joyful over wrong.

Of course, Paul didn't stop with a list of negatives but went on to delineate that love (1) is patient, (2) is kind, (3) rejoices in the right, (4) bears all things, (5) believes all things, (6) hopes all things, and (7) endures all things.

Paul explains that such unselfish love comes to us only as the gift of God, for man's love is inherently selfish. That's why love is rare in our world today. Everyone wants it, but most people go to the wrong source to find it. Those who are guilty of calling a spade a steam shovel have misdirected them. They do not understand that before they can show this kind of love, God has to change their hearts.

The Bible tells us that in the Garden of Eden God planted two special trees. He designed the tree of life as the source from which man could perpetuate his life forever as long as he had access to its fruit. The other tree offered a means by which man could exercise his freedom of choice; it was known as the tree of knowledge of good and evil. If man ate of its fruit, he would learn from experience the bitter results of disobedience.

Since Adam and Eve both flunked the test, mankind now knows all too much about evil. Genuine love has become alien to human nature. God gave the capacity for love to man and wife in the beginning, but it has become commercialized and equated with the pornographic—the basis of all that is cheap, tawdry, and disgusting.

Calling a Spade a Steam Shovel

People are beginning to realize that Hollywood and the gross exploitation of sex in our society have cheated them. *Time* magazine published a cover story in January, 1973, on the notorious film *Last Tango in Paris* that seemed to crystallize the indignation that's been building up over the exploitation of sex. The publishers expected a few irate letters to their own blatant buildup of that movie, but they were overwhelmed with bushel basketfuls of them and furious cancellations of subscriptions. What surprised and hurt the editors most, however, was that they lost thousands of dollars' worth of ads from disapproving advertisers.

Typical of the irate letters received are the following, which tell us something about people's disillusionment with the exploitation of sex:

From a reader in Bayonne, New Jersey, came this classic: "Sir/Minutes after my *Time* came, I threw it in the refuse can, whereupon the rest of the garbage got out and walked away."

From Coos Bay, Oregon, came the following thought-provoking analysis: "Sir/Your cover story on *Last Tango* (Jan. 22) terrified me. A society that spends so much time thinking about, filming and writing about sex obviously does not have much else it considers important enough to occupy it.

"We are now nearly ready for the takeover, from wherever it may come. We have not the mental vigor left to resist, and someone will walk off with the house while we are preoccupied in the bedroom."

Amid predictions of dire results to come was this one from Richland, Michigan: "Sir/Those of us who are awaiting the reformation must be grate-

God's Footprint on My Floor

ful to Marlon Brando and Director Bertolucci.

"Only after respectable folk embrace the excesses of an era can a return to decency begin."

In order to straighten out the love relationship that God fully intended to be a blessing and a bond between human beings, we must first of all have a loving relationship with Him. God longs for us to experience genuine love, for it is basic to our whole Christian relationship.

Henry Drummond had great talents in science and mathematics, but as a young man he entered the ministry in Scotland. While at the peak of his abilities and in the full ardor of his love for Christ, he prepared a sermon entitled "The Greatest Thing in the World." Drummond's sermon was such a masterpiece that it was soon printed throughout the Christian world. In this masterful sermon, Drummond asked, "Why is love greater than faith? Because the end is greater than the means." He went on to illustrate that love is the fulfilling of the law. It's just as you would say to a man who loves his wife with all tenderness, "You are at liberty to beat her, hurt her, kill her if you want to." He just naturally *won't want* to. If we really love, it is preposterous to say to us, "Do not kill." It is insulting to suggest, "Do not steal." It is un- necessary to beg, "Please do not bear false witness against your neighbor." The last thing we would want to do would be to covet that which is our neighbors'.

Yet somehow, and very gradually over the years, Drummond's interest in a liberal, scientific ap- proach to religion led him away from a sense of

Calling a Spade a Steam Shovel

personal commitment. One day it came as a shock for him to realize that he had drifted far away from the simple, loving faith he had once known. The resulting inner turmoil was aggravated by the news that he was suffering from an incurable illness. To his friend Sir William Dawson, Henry Drummond announced, "I'm going back to the Bible." As he reread 1 Corinthians 13 and then his own thinking on it as revealed in his sermon "The Greatest Thing in the World," he fell in love with Christ again. His sermon had saved his own spiritual life, and in the few remaining months of his life he declared, "Ten minutes spent in Christ's company every morning, aye, two minutes, if it be face to Face and heart to Heart, will change the whole day."

The expression "new morality" often describes wife-swapping, skinny-dipping, pregnant high school girls, homosexuality, abortion, violence, lying, cheating, chiseling, criminal neglect of the aged and needy, and a host of other actions and attitudes once called into question by our traditional moral principles. However, it's really nothing more than the old dragon of sin rearing its ugly head.

Although people attend church as much, if not more, than ever before, today's church is losing its influence when it comes to setting moral standards. It seems that the church, for the most part, is as confused as the rest of society about how to deal with the tough moral issues of our time.

Yet amid all this confusion and clamor, Jesus' voice of authority points the way: "Blessed are the pure in heart: for they shall see God" (Matthew 5:8).

God's Footprint on My Floor

"Into the city of God there will enter nothing that defiles. All who are to be dwellers there will here have become pure in heart. In one who is learning of Jesus, there will be manifest a growing distaste for careless manners, unseemly language, and coarse thought. When Christ abides in the heart, there will be purity and refinement of thought and manner.

"But the words of Jesus, 'Blessed are the pure in heart,' have a deeper meaning—not merely pure in the sense in which the world understands purity, free from that which is sensual, pure from lust, but true in the hidden purposes and motives of the soul, free from pride and self-seeking, humble, unselfish, childlike" (*Thoughts From the Mount of Blessing*, p. 25).

We can't live like that on our own, of course. But the apostle Paul testified in Philippians 4:13, "I can do all things through Christ which strengtheneth me." We turn again to *Thoughts From the Mount of Blessing* to find out exactly how this works. "But to hearts that have become purified through the indwelling of the Holy Spirit, all is changed. These can know God. Moses was hid in the cleft of the rock when the glory of the Lord was revealed to him; and it is when we are hid in Christ that we behold the love of God.

" 'He that loveth pureness of heart, for the grace of his lips the King shall be his friend.' Proverbs 22:11. By faith we behold Him here and now. In our daily experience we discern His goodness and compassion in the manifestation of His providence. We recognize Him in the character of His Son. The

Calling a Spade a Steam Shovel

Holy Spirit takes the truth concerning God and Him whom He hath sent, and opens it to the understanding and to the heart. The pure in heart see God in a new and endearing relation, as their Redeemer; and while they discern the purity and loveliness of His character, they long to reflect His image. They see Him as a Father longing to embrace a repenting son, and their hearts are filled with joy unspeakable and full of glory" (page 26).

When the power of Christ's life is placed at our disposal, we not only *can* become but *must be* pure in heart. The impossible becomes possible through Christ's grace. But we too have our part to play. "The work of gaining salvation is one of copartnership, a joint operation. There is to be co-operation between God and the repentant sinner.... Man is to make earnest efforts to overcome that which hinders him from attaining to perfection. But he is wholly dependent upon God for success. Human effort of itself is not sufficient. Without the aid of divine power it avails nothing. . . . Resistance of temptation must come from man, who must draw his power from God. On the one side there is infinite wisdom, compassion, and power; on the other, weakness, sinfulness, absolute helplessness.

"God wishes us to have the mastery over ourselves. But He cannot help us without our consent and co-operation. . . . Of ourselves, we are not able to bring the purposes and desires and inclinations into harmony with the will of God; but if we are 'willing to be made willing,' the Saviour will accomplish this for us" (Ellen G. White, *The Acts of the Apostles,* p. 482).

God's Footprint on My Floor

Have you ever noticed that when a married couple follow the so-called old-fashioned moral tradition and live together for a number of years that they come to act and look alike? Similarly, the more we live with Jesus, the more we will become like Him.

The apostle John, when he first became acquainted with Jesus, was known as a "son of thunder" because of his impulsive nature and fiery temper. Even after he'd been with Jesus awhile, he wanted to call fire from heaven to burn up a town that refused to accept Jesus. But John's life gradually changed through his association with Christ. "The depth and fervor of John's affection for his Master was not the cause of Christ's love for him, but the effect of that love. John desired to become like Jesus, and under the transforming influence of the love of Christ he did become meek and lowly. Self was hid in Jesus. Above all his companions, John yielded himself to the power of that wondrous life. He says, 'The life was manifested, and we have seen it.' 'And of His fullness have we all received, and grace for grace.' 1 John 1:2; John 1:16. John knew the Saviour by an experimental knowledge. His Master's lessons were graven upon his soul. When he testified of the Saviour's grace, his simple language was eloquent with the love that pervaded his whole being" (ibid., pp. 544, 545).

John became one of Jesus' dearest friends and constant companions. Jesus chose John to be with Him at His transfiguration and to pray with Him in Gethsemane. John, a personal acquaintance of

Calling a Spade a Steam Shovel

Caiaphas (the high priest), was allowed to witness Jesus' trial. Thus he recorded for us all the details of that unjust episode. John followed Jesus to Pilate's judgment hall, and his heart must have been broken there by the ridicule and violence heaped on the Master he loved. Finally John followed the crowd to Golgotha where he watched soldiers drive nails through Jesus' hands and feet. John knew more about the love of Jesus than any other man because he allowed the love and companionship of Jesus to change his personality. And that same love and companionship which so wonderfully changed John's life can change our lives too.

Words can only inadequately express Christ's love and His desire to be our Friend and Companion. He has walked the way of life before us. He was tempted in all points in which we are tempted. Never once yielding to sin, He overcame sin and death for us. He is by our sides now, with His arm of love about us. He is whispering in our ears, "I want to be your Friend. I love you as no one else ever has or ever can. I want to help you heavenward to the mansions I've prepared for you."

We can respond to His love by saying, "Yes, Jesus, I want to be your friend. I want to live so close to You that I will become more like You every day."

God's Footprint on My Floor

CHRIST'S ANSWER TO MAN'S NEED
(Based on the Beatitudes in Matthew 5)

OUR PROBLEM	CHRIST'S ANSWER	RESULTS
1. PRIDE INSECURITY POOR SELF-IMAGE	(Blessed are . . .) *THE POOR IN SPIRIT Those who recognize their need and begin to do something about it	*Acceptance of self *Conquest of false pride *Meaningful communion with God and man
2. SIN AND GUILT	*THEY THAT MOURN Repentance for and turning from sin	*Clear conscience *Evidence of acceptance by God and man
3. REBELLIOUSNESS, ANGER, LACK OF CONFIDENCE	*THE MEEK Submissiveness and dedication to the will of God for us	*Acceptance of authority *Development of trust and confidence in God and man
4. UNHAPPINESS, FEAR, FRUSTRATION, WORRY	*THEY WHICH DO HUNGER AND THIRST AFTER RIGHTEOUS-NESS Filled with the Water of life—justification	*Healthy emotions *Wholistic development *Right with God and man
5. BITTERNESS AND SELFISHNESS	*THE MERCIFUL Forgiving attitude, willingness to share, spiritual growth	*Improvement of relationships *Identification, sharing *Love to God and man
6. IMPURITY AND IMMORALITY	*THE PURE IN HEART Cleanliness, purity, integrity in life	*Moral freedom *Law of God in heart *Right doing toward God and man
7. DESPAIR AND APATHY	*THE PEACEMAKERS Exude peace, happiness, content-ment; share these with all with whom you come in contact THESE ARE THE SEVEN STEPS WE MUST TAKE IN ORDER TO BECOME SONS AND DAUGH-TERS OF GOD	*Peace that passes understanding *Portrayal of God to man

Chapter 9

Mother Mud and Father Fear

Julian Huxley, in his book *Man Stands Alone,* pictures the human race as a curious by-product of a universe utterly indifferent to its life and even to its presence. This bleak philosophy—the natural outgrowth of the evolutionistic-humanistic dogma —has led to the fear, hopelessness, and despair that characterize many thinking men of our age.

Young people particularly have grown up without anything to believe in; they are lost in the whirlpool of uncertainty. They have searched along many promising paths for some certainty or truth, only to find that these are but blind alleys. Many stumble hopefully down the popular paths of wealth, pleasure, fame, and power, only to grow frustrated and disappointed.

One of the brightest paths of our time has been that marked "Education." Thousands have traveled it with eager, expectant feet, but where has it led them? Although their heads are crammed full of knowledge, often their souls are spiritual vacuums.

On top of this, ever since the atomic age began at Hiroshima, we have lived in a perpetual crisis atmosphere so terrifying, so universal, and so altogether unprecedented that it has numbed men's minds.

Jules Moch of France describes the devastating threats of our age this way: Today "not one but a thousand swords of Damocles dangle over us" (quoted by A. S. Maxwell in *Courage for the Crisis*, p. 2).

This century which was touted back in the thirties as the "Century of Progress," technologically has more than met its promise. What, then, has taken the golden sheen off our age of promise, progress, and plenty? Man has accepted himself as the son of Mother Mud. Evolution and humanism can lead only to fear, frustration, and despair, because man cannot lift himself out of the mire of sin by his own bootstraps.

Indeed, the greatest evidence of what's basically wrong with the theory of evolution is seen in the results of its promulgation for over one hundred years. Mother Mud is linked inevitably with Father Fear. But not only to fear. Many years ago some perceptive college youths recognized the implications of the theory of evolution and organized an atheists' club on their campus which took as its slogan: "Sons of apes don't need a Saviour." Truly if we are not the sons of God, there are no permanent moral values.

The last part of the Book of Judges had always been difficult for me to explain until I found what I believe to be the key to understanding it. Judges records some of the ugliest incidents found in the Scriptures. Even in our so-called enlightened age we are shocked when we read about them. But

Mother Mud and Father Fear

then I realized that this section is located between two scriptures which tell us: "In those days there was no king in Israel, but every man did that which was right in his own eyes" (Judges 17:6; see also 21:25).

The proponents of the new morality claim that they have found *freedom,* but they don't seem to understand what freedom is really all about. Freedom is *not* doing just what we want to do. Suppose everyone had that idea of freedom. Suppose college students were to sit up all night cramming for final exams, as they sometimes do, and stumble bleary-eyed into class the next morning prepared to do or die, but the professor doesn't show up. He's decided he has academic freedom, and he doesn't come to class because he doesn't want to. But those students waiting anxiously to get the exam over with as soon as possible wouldn't consider that academic freedom at all. They'd call it *irresponsibility.*

The same reasoning can apply to all society. Bus drivers, following the concept that each man has a right to do his own thing, would show up for work only when they felt like it. Druggists, grocers, doctors, policemen, and airline pilots are all *free* men and women too. They could all take the same attitude we've been describing, but this wouldn't be freedom. It would be anarchy.

What is freedom? True freedom comes only from placing oneself fully in accord with the Creator's laws, which He designed for the full, happy, and peaceful operation of our universe. The book *Patriarchs and Prophets,* page 34, tells us: "The law of love being the foundation of the government of God, the happiness of all intelligent beings depends upon their perfect accord with its great principles of righteousness."

The same holds true in the laws of health as well. Most of us don't really get concerned about our health until we lose it—then we search for some remedy that will quickly get our bodies back in good running condition so that we can begin again those pet, but harmful, habits which caused our body to malfunction in the first place. In the long run we lose out on life—several years of it —and also fail to get the most out of what we do have.

We can illustrate the point by going back to the record of Creation found in the Book of Genesis. The first thing God created was light, yet our main source of light, the sun, provides more than light. "There are but few who realize that, in order to enjoy health and cheerfulness, they must have an abundance of sunlight, pure air, and physical exercise. . . .

"Go out into the light and warmth of the glorious sun . . . and share with vegetation its life-giving, healing power. . . .

"If you would have your homes sweet and inviting, make them bright with air and sunshine. . . . The precious sunlight may fade your carpets, but it will give a healthful color to the cheeks of your children. . . .

"Exercise and a free abundant use of the air and sunlight—blessings which Heaven has freely bestowed upon all—would give life and strength"

Mother Mud and Father Fear

(Ellen G. White, *My Life Today,* p. 138).

We need sunshine in our souls too. "A mind can be such a happy place when the shades are up and we look out into the future unafraid. But when the shades are tightly drawn, and the doubt-colored light falls upon the wrong thought patterns papering the walls of the soul, it's a dismal place. All too soon it becomes a deep, dark cavern where its tormented inmate sees no light in the universe, and doubts that any exists" (Marjorie Lewis Lloyd, *This Thing Called Fear,* p. 11). We need to throw open the windows of the soul and let the sunshine of God's love dispel the gloom and fear and despair.

The Beatitude around which this chapter centers explains it this way: "Blessed are the peacemakers: for they shall be called the children of God." That's it. We've arrived! We're truly children of God when we become peacemakers, but to be peacemakers we, first of all, must have His peace in our lives. Now, God doesn't do away with all the fearful things about us, but He does give us a confident trust in His goodness and love so that we can face a world of fear calmly and peacefully. The apostle Paul faced many enemies and trials, but he testified from his own experience, "And the peace of God, *which passeth all understanding,* shall keep your hearts and minds through Christ Jesus" (Philippians 4:7).

Among His parting words to His followers Jesus promised, "Peace I leave with you, my peace I give unto you: not as the world giveth, give I unto you. Let not your heart be troubled, neither let it be afraid" (John 14:27).

God's Footprint on My Floor

As Prince of peace Christ restores to earth and heaven the peace that sin has disrupted. "Being justified by faith, we have peace with God through our Lord Jesus Christ" (Romans 5:1). Whenever we decide to renounce our sin and open our hearts to Christ's love, we just naturally partake of this heavenly peace.

Strangely, some are afraid even of yielding themselves to the Prince of peace, but as Marjorie Lewis Lloyd explains, "There is no risk in surrender. God is not standing over us with a list of terrible calamities and requirements, ready to tumble them upon us the moment we surrender completely. There is no risk in it.

"It is no more dangerous to make a complete surrender to God than for a baby to fall asleep in its mother's arms. That's pretty risky, isn't it? The mother might trip and fall. Or there might be a fire, or an automobile accident.

"But with God there's no risk at all. . . .

" 'It is safe to let go every earthly support, and take the hand of Him who lifted up and saved the sinking disciple on the stormy sea.'

"One of the most tormenting fears is the fear of making a complete surrender. And 'fear hath torment.' Oh, if only we could know what surrender really is, and what it is not. Surrender is not telling God to go ahead with all the terrible things He has in mind for us. Surrender is just knowing that God loves us. It's as simple as that!" (ibid., p. 17).

Previously in this chapter we mentioned the light which God created at the beginning of Creation Week and likened it to the light of His presence

Mother Mud and Father Fear

that fills our souls and displaces the darkness of gloom and despair. Now let's briefly look at His concluding act of Creation Week to learn about another symbol of the peace and rest which He gives.

When God created our world, He provided a plan by which all creation could periodically experience in a special way the peace and happiness of heaven. At the end of the sixth day of this first week as the evening sun quietly placed its benediction upon the fresh, new world and slipped beneath the horizon, the Genesis record tells us that God rested.

Rested? Why would God rest? Did the tremendous energy involved in the work of creating the earth and sea and sky sap God's strength? Of course not. God rested on the seventh day as an example for man—to demonstrate that each week we can rest from our labors and enjoy the peace and happiness which come from special communion with the Creator. Such rest is not merely physical. It involves the mental, social, and spiritual faculties too. The Sabbath is not so much a period of rest from wearing toil as it is an attitude of confidence, trust, and happiness in the Creator. "Confident in the power of your Creator, you trust Him to do a work of re-creation in your life, to make a saint out of a sinner. You commit your life to the love of 'a Faithful Creator,' trusting Him to weave into His perfect tapestry the threads of your experience. That is rest. That is peace.

"The Sabbath is an antidote for fear, for true Sabbathkeeping knows no fear" (ibid., p. 43).

God's Footprint on My Floor

The Jews have a long and unbroken history of keeping the seventh-day Sabbath, and Rabbi Abraham Heschel beautifully explains the Jewish understanding of the Sabbath in these words: "The meaning of the Sabbath is to celebrate time rather than space. Six days a week we live under the tyranny of the things of space; on the Sabbath we try to become attuned to *holiness in time*. It is a day on which we are called upon to share in what is eternal in time, to turn from the results of creation to the mystery of creation; from the world of creation to the creation of the world. . . . Six days a week we wrestle with the world, wringing profit from the earth; on the Sabbath we especially care for the seed of eternity planted in the soul. . . . It is not an interlude but the climax of living. . . . The seventh day is a *palace in time* which we build. It is made of soul, of joy and reticence. . . . The art of keeping the seventh day is the art of painting on a canvas of time the mysterious grandeur of the climax of creation: as He sanctified the seventh day, so shall we. The love of the Sabbath is the love of man for what he and God have in common. Our keeping the Sabbath day is a paraphrase of His sanctification of the seventh day. What would be a world without Sabbath? It would be a world that knew only itself or God distorted as a thing or the abyss separating Him from the world; a world without the vision of a window in eternity that opens into time" (*The Sabbath,* pp. 10-16).

But we must not hoard the peace God gives us. Our Beatitude does not place its blessing on those

Mother Mud and Father Fear

who experience peace but those who are *peace-makers.* "Christ's followers are sent to the world with the message of peace. Whoever, by the quiet, unconscious influence of a holy life, shall reveal the love of Christ; whoever, by word or deed, shall lead another to renounce sin and yield his heart to God, is a peacemaker.

"And 'blessed are the peacemakers: for they shall be called the children of God.' The spirit of peace is evidence of their connection with heaven. The sweet savor of Christ surrounds them. The fragrance of the life, the loveliness of the character, reveal to the world the fact that they are children of God. Men take knowledge of them that they have been with Jesus" (*Thoughts From the Mount of Blessing,* p. 28).

A strangely contradictory statement seems to follow in Matthew 5. Somehow we have the idea that peace is the absence of strife, hardship, and trouble. But that's only a shallow kind of peace —the peace-at-any-price philosophy. Jesus pointed out that the children of God have a peace which comes from a strong confidence and sense of security in a loving God who will provide for them no matter what happens. Thus He adds a blessing for the sake of those who have become children of God so that they might know that in the inevitable results of living for Christ, the hand of a loving Father is still at work:

"Blessed are they which are persecuted for righteousness' sake: for their's is the kingdom of heaven. Blessed are ye, when men shall revile you, and persecute you, and shall say all manner of evil against you falsely, for my sake. Rejoice, and be exceeding glad: for great is your reward in heaven: for so persecuted they the prophets which were before you" (Matthew 5:10-12).

We might respond, "Well, that's small comfort! Just because the prophets were persecuted, why should I be?" But Jesus was the greatest of the prophets, and none of them suffered as He did. The gospel hymnwriter Thomas Shepherd asks, "Must Jesus bear the cross alone, and all the world go free?" And he responds, "No, there's a cross for everyone"—a cross for you, a cross for me.

Jesus does not present His children with the hope of having a life free from trial. Instead He offers us the privilege of walking with Him in the pathway of self-denial and reproach. But He does promise us the strength to bear His cross and to share His humiliation.

And there's a hidden purpose in it all. "Through trials and persecution, the glory—character—of God is revealed in His chosen ones. The church of God, hated and persecuted by the world, are educated and disciplined in the school of Christ. They walk in narrow paths on earth; they are purified in the furnace of affliction. They follow Christ through sore conflicts; they endure self-denial and experience bitter disappointments; but their painful experience teaches them the guilt and woe of sin, and they look upon it with abhorrence. Being partakers of Christ's sufferings, they are destined to be partakers of His glory" (*Thoughts From the Mount of Blessing,* p. 31).

Did you ever stop to think that one reason God

allows persecution is so that others may marvel at the peace which characterizes God's children even when they're wrongfully abused? There's something different about one who doesn't retaliate.

Jesus illustrates the effectiveness of the true Christian's witness by likening it in Matthew 5: 13-16 to the salt of the earth and the light of the world. He challenges, "Let your light so shine before men, that they may see your good works, and glorify your Father which is in heaven" (verse 16).

This isn't *our* light. It's His. The beauty and glory of the sunshine of His love and character have filled our souls to the place where it overflows to those about us. The prophet Isaiah saw that this would be the result when he commanded, "Arise, shine; for thy light is come, and the glory of the Lord is risen upon thee. For, behold, the darkness shall cover the earth, and gross darkness the people: but the Lord *shall arise* upon thee, and *his glory* shall be seen upon thee" (Isaiah 60:1, 2).

And what is the response of a world wrapped in gloom and despair? "And the Gentiles shall come to thy light, and kings to the brightness of thy rising" (verse 3).

It has to begin somewhere and with someone, however. And it can begin here and now with you and me. The Creator's voice commands, "Let there be light!" And may there be, as the darkness of our souls is filled with the light of His presence. "Arise, shine; for thy light is come." Let the glory of the Lord be seen upon you, and let His footprint be seen upon your floor.

God's Footprint on My Floor

Chapter 10

Two Tables of Ten

Two tables of ten—given by God Himself. Two tables of ten—outlining what it truly means to live Christlike lives. Two tables of ten—the mirror of our Christian experience. But more than that—much, more!

Actually the two tables which make up what is known as the Ten Commandments are two tables of promise. Not of promise as to what man can do, but of what God makes it possible for us to do by His grace if we'll only let Him have His way in our lives. It isn't, then, what we do but what Christ does when we allow Him to live out His life within us.

We have explained the Beatitudes as progressive steps in becoming children of God. They demonstrate how He leads us step by step in achieving what He has already made possible for us to achieve. However, Satan wants to keep us from understanding the purpose of the law and from seeing its promise. In fact, he has tried from the inception of sin to convince the entire universe that created beings cannot live according to God's law.

But Christ came to prove just the opposite. He

119

demonstrated in His life and death what it means
to actually fulfill the law. Jesus came to bring us
a new perspective of the purpose, power, and promise of God's law.

Sometimes we assume that God's laws are arbitrary regulations imposed on us in order to keep
us in line. But they are really evidences of His
loving concern. God is interested in every phase
of our being—in the way we eat, sleep, dress, and
play, as well as in the way we worship. He wants
us to get the most out of life *now* as well as to enjoy
the blessings of immortality in the world soon to
come. Our happiness, then, depends on our full
cooperation with these laws and, of course, on careful study of their guidelines. "His laws are not
arbitrary exactions. Every 'Thou shalt not,' whether
in physical or moral law, contains or implies a
promise. If it is obeyed, blessings will attend our
steps; if it is disobeyed, the result is danger and
unhappiness" (Ellen G. White, *Healthful Living*,
p. 18).

Part of our problem is that our perspective is
too limited, and thus we settle for little when God
makes much possible. We really can and need to
become experts in demonstrating the beauty and
goodness of God's law in our daily lives.

Pastor Walter Ogura tells a story which cleverly
illustrates this point. A young oil salesman in the
days of feudal Japan passed by an old *soko* (ware-
house). Hearing some strange sounds inside, he
peered through a crack in the wall and was fasci-
nated to see some young *samurai* (the feudal
knights of Japan) shooting arrows at targets inside

God's Footprint on My Floor

the building. They thought no one could watch them there, for they were just learning the skill. Some weren't even hitting the target, let alone the bull's-eye, and the salesman couldn't help but burst out laughing at their lack of expertise.

The *samurai* heard his laughter and, being offended, rushed out of the *soko* and grabbed him. "So you're laughing at us," they screamed. "Well, if you think you can do any better, come and show us. If you can't, we'll fix you for being so disrespectful."

He was on the spot and had to think quickly. "Honestly," he replied, "I've never shot an arrow in my life. But I still have every right to laugh at you."

"How come?" they demanded.

"You see, shooting arrows isn't my line. That's yours. But I'm able to do very well in my line, so I have a right to laugh when you don't do very well in yours."

While saying this, he took out a coin which had a square hole in the center and held it in front of him. Then he took a bottle of his lamp oil, held it at arm's length above his head, and without looking at the bottle poured the oil so accurately and in such a light stream that it all ran right through the hole in the coin.

He so impressed the young *samurai* with his skill that they let him go.

When I heard Pastor Ogura tell the story, he pointed out that we must not only set our goals for ourselves but also be able to hit our targets. Actually, in our Christian lives God sets the goals, high goals.

Two Tables of Ten

But He also makes it possible for every one of us to achieve them. When we take the name Christian we are taking His name in vain unless we lead the kind of lives His transforming grace makes possible.

Of course God doesn't expect us to fully reproduce the character of Christ all at once in our lives any more than we'd expect neophyte *samurai* to always hit the target with their arrows, or even the Japanese oil salesman to accomplish his spectacular stunt the very first time he tried it. He gives His grace to us to grow by, and He expects that we will continually grow toward the goals He has set.

Some of us have used the phrase "righteousness by faith" so long and so glibly that we have come to believe that our righteousness *is* accomplished *by* our faith. It isn't at all. Ellen G. White plainly tells us, "There is nothing in faith that makes it our saviour. Faith cannot remove our guilt. Christ is the power of God unto salvation to all them that believe" (*Seventh-day Adventist Bible Commentary,* Vol. 6, p. 1071). The Scriptures explain clearly: "*By* grace are ye saved *through* faith" (Ephesians 2:8).

Grace includes more than justification. It embraces God's transforming action in our lives. It is God doing for us that which we in no way can ever hope to do for ourselves. Faith cannot save us; it can only reach out and appropriate that which God has already accomplished.

Christ's kind of righteousness so far exceeds anything man can imagine or achieve by his own

God's Footprint on My Floor

physical, mental, or spiritual faculties that there is no possibility at all of any of us ever reaching the goals God sets by *anything* we can do. Our *faith* cannot accomplish it for us any more than our *works* can, although both are, of course, part of God's plan by which we appropriate the merits of Christ. Faith accepts what He has done for us, and the works are evidenced in us as fruit of the Spirit. What Jesus did make crystal clear in the Sermon on the Mount is that the humblest, weakest, and poorest of us can achieve the magnificent results of His working in us as outlined in this book. By His transforming grace and power we can produce lives which characterize the sons and daughters of God.

God's two tables of ten, in His plan, become the mirrors which point out how far short we fall of being saved to the uttermost. Yet they are more than that. They represent God's call and challenge to us to come up higher still to a plane of holy living we've probably never considered possible.

I came across the following in a church bulletin: "Select a large box and fill it to capacity with cannonballs. When it is full, bring a quantity of marbles. Many of these can easily fit into the spaces between the cannonballs. The box is full, but only in a sense. There is space in abundance into which you can place buckshot. Now the box is full beyond question. It will not hold another cannonball, another marble, or even more buckshot. Yet several pounds of sand can be poured into the box, and even then you could find ample room for several jugs of water." Whoever it was that wrote out the illustra-

Two Tables of Ten

tion concluded: "The full capacity of man has not been reached."

That's really what the two tables of ten are all about. That's what the perfect life of Jesus demonstrates to us. Our full capacity has yet to be reached. God is still waiting for His people to take Him at His word. For too long we have thought of God's two tables of ten as only being ten *commandments*. But we need to see them for what they really are —ten great *promises*—promises of what God fully intends to accomplish in our lives.

It will take total commitment to His will on our part. Only as we completely surrender ourselves to Him can the power and purpose of His promises be evident in transformed, victorious lives and in unselfish, loving service to those about us. The inhabitants of our world today, more than ever before, desperately seek for this kind of evidence—the handwriting of God in our hearts that enables us to leave His footprint on their floor.